MW01233487

THE
PROPHETIC
FUTURE
CONCEALED
in
Israel's
FESTIVALS

PERRY STONE

THE
PROPHETIC
FUTURE
CONCEALED

in
Israel's

FESTIVALS

THE PROPHETIC FUTURE CONCEALED IN ISRAEL'S FESTIVALS
Published by: The International Offices of Voice of Evangelism Ministries
P. O. Box 3595
Cleveland, TN 37320
www.voe.org
423.478.3456

Scripture quotations without notation are from the King James Version of the Bible.

Scripture quotations marked NKJV are from the New King James Version of the Bible. Copyright © 1979, 1980, 1982 by Thomas Nelson, Inc., publishers. Used by permission.

Copyright © 2013 by Perry F. Stone, Jr.
ISBN 978-0-9708611-9-1
First Edition Printing 2013
Cover design by Michael Dutton
Printed in the United States of America

CONTENTS

INTRODUCTION

Many years ago, I was sitting across the table in a restaurant with one of the noted men of God of our day. He had served as a national youth leader, as president of a major college, and as presiding Bishop of a major church denomination. He is known as one of America's outstanding ministers of the Gospel. He and I were discussing the so-called controversial aspects of my Hebraic teaching. One of my questions to him concerned why I received harsh criticism from some of my own brethren over certain messages I preached, especially those dealing with the Hebraic roots of the Christian faith.

He said, "Perry, you preach extensively on Biblical types and shadows, and how they were fulfilled through Christ. Your research is strong in Old Testament teaching. Many ministers, including myself, do not often preach types and shadows, but preach a more expository form of message. When church members watch you on television or hear you teach, they often ask their pastor for his comment regarding something they have heard. Instead of saying, 'You should contact Brother Stone and ask him,' it is easier to say, 'I don't agree with what he is preaching,' or 'he preaches outside of the Bible.' At times they do this to cover for their lack of knowledge and Biblical research.

"Then word gets out that you are preaching things that people do not agree with, and some will go so far as to say that your teaching has no Biblical foundation. It is simply ignorance of the information that causes the criticism."

From years of comments I had heard from certain critics, I knew that he was correct in that assessment.

I was raised in a Christian family, with a father who served as an evangelist before I was born. By the time I was born, he was pastoring a church. Growing up in church and having other ministers in the family, I recall that the majority of the sermons I heard were from the New Testament, and many from the four gospels. Of course these were powerful and faith building. Yet, I seldom heard teaching from the thirty-nine books of the Old Testament, unless it was to relate a story that had some practical application for believers today. This was not due to a lack of study from ministers, but a lack of understanding of the importance of the Hebraic, Old Testament roots of the Christian faith.

Believers always spoke of Easter, but never the true term for the season—Passover—which is the Biblical name of the important feast commemorating the death of Christ. Each year, ministers in our denomination spoke of Pentecost Sunday, probably because our church was classified as a Pentecostal, Full Gospel church. However, I cannot recall hearing a teaching on the Feast of Trumpets, the Day of Atonement or Tabernacles—three of Israel's fall feasts. Why is that?

For some reason many of our ministers never studied the Bible from a Hebraic perspective, as they saw no purpose in teaching or understanding Old Testament information. To some the Old Testament represented the law and we were "not under the law," thus why preach something they thought had passed away or been replaced. I also believe they did not understand the *shadow* of those things that were made *substance* in the sufferings and redemptive work of Christ.

By not understanding and teaching this, I personally think we missed out on one of the most interesting aspects of study from the Torah (which is the name for the first five books of the Bible that God gave to Moses). Those books contain much insight into God's code of future events, especially those linked to the three fall feasts. In the feasts we find the *gathering together* (called the Rapture), the *tribulation*, and the *future Messianic kingdom*.

With an explosion of interest in Hebraic teaching, and being one of the early teachers of the subject as far back as 1986, I felt a need to give a detailed explanation of the purpose of the festivals (or feasts) and their application, as well as an explanation of how three of these feasts will be prophetically fulfilled in the future. I believe you will glean powerful insight into this subject as you learn how precisely God established His types and shadows of things to come!

This study will explore how the order of Israel's Fall Feasts also encodes the proper order of future prophetic events. This will help settle the debate about the timing of the Rapture, and whether it is before, during, or after the coming seven-year tribulation. Many answers are found in the Torah, as we study the Biblical types and shadows of the inspired Word of God.

Be Blessed with Understanding!
Perry Stone, Jr.

Chapter 1

THE CODES ARE HIDDEN IN THE SHADOWS

The Apostle Paul, writing in Colossians 2:16-17, said that the Sabbaths, new moons and holy days were a shadow of things to come: *"So let no one judge you in food or in drink, or regarding a festival or a new moon or Sabbaths, which are a shadow of things to come, but the substance is of Christ."* The Sabbaths initiated rest cycles for Israel—every seven days, every seventh year, and every forty-nine years, in which the fiftieth year was a jubilee cycle (Lev. 23 and 25). New moons were the monthly cycles of the renewal of the moon. When the sliver of the moon was identified, the next Jewish month would begin.

The Lord's holy festivals in the Torah consisted of seven major feasts of Israel, and later other national celebrations were recognized to commemorate major spiritual and political events linked with the Jewish people. All of these festivals were shadows of future events.

A shadow is not the *actual image* of the thing, but it reveals the *form* of the object. Later the true light reveals the actual object itself. Before we move into the *shadow* to gain insight on the *substance*, we need to understand the meaning of specific terms used in the Bible. We must understand how the Old Testament is the New Testament concealed, and the New Testament is the Old Testament revealed.

WHAT IS A TYPE?

In Biblical theology, scholars speak of something being a type or a shadow. The word *type* is derived from the Greek word *tupos*, and is found sixteen times in the New Testament. It is translated in the King James Version of the Bible as print (John 20:25), figure (Rom. 5:14), pattern (Heb. 8:5), manner (Acts 23:25), a form (Rom. 6:17), and example (1 Cor. 10:6, 11). An Old Testament *type* is a person, place, thing, or event that resembles a person, place, thing, or event in the New Testament. The *type* is not the original, but a preview of the original.

The word shadow is the Greek word *skia* (Col. 2:17). A shadow is an imperfect image or copy that is a reflection of the true substance. Just like with your own shadow, a shadow is the *reflection* of light that is cast upon the actual object.

A shadow prefigures the anti-type (the anti-type being the later person or thing that fulfilled the shadow). Paul used the word *shadow* in Hebrews 10:1, "For the law having a shadow of good things to come..." A shadow implies that the reality is yet to come, but a reflection of what is to come is found in the past, or in the shadow.

Concealed within the Law was the reality of events and stories of the coming Messiah. The Old Testament holds the shadow; the New Testament removes the shadow and brings forth the light.

The term copy, or *pattern,* is the Greek word *hupodeigma*, a word that speaks to *a sketch of something in the future.* For example, the Tabernacle furniture and priestly services were a pattern of things to come in Christ. The sacred furniture was actually patterned after the sacred furniture found in the Heavenly Temple (see Heb. 8:5). Not every prophetic narrative in the Old Testament classifies as a type, shadow, or pattern of things to come. However, there are many types and shadows found in the Tabernacle, the priesthood, the sacrifices, and the priestly ministry.

WHAT IS AN ANTI-TYPE?

A theological phrase called *the anti-type* is the fulfillment of the type or shadow. From a Biblical standpoint, the type is concealed in the

Old Testament and the anti-type is revealed in the New Testament. Before the act of final redemption on the cross, Christ compared His future suffering to the story of Jonah being in the belly of the fish for three days and nights: *"For as Jonas was three days and three nights in the whale's belly; so shall the Son of man be three days and three nights in the heart of the earth"* (Matt. 12:40). In certain catacombs of Rome, large whales are carved on the outer entrances as a sign of the promise of the resurrection of the righteous. Both Jonah and Christ were brought forth after three days.

Another anti-type was the sacrifice of Isaac on the altar on Mount Moriah, which was a foreshadowing of the crucifixion of Christ (see Gen 22). From Mount Moriah in Jerusalem, God provided a *ram* for Abraham; and through Christ, God provided a *Lamb* for the world!

Another beautiful imagery is in the story of Joseph and how he provided salvation for his brothers through his own season of suffering—a portrait of Christ's suffering at the hands of his own people.

Numerous types are found throughout the Scriptures. For example, the first Adam in the garden is a type of Christ. And Christ, who is called the "last Adam," also experienced agony in Gethsemane's garden (Luke 22: 44). Thus we have two Adams, neither created through a normal conception process. The first Adam was created fully grown, while Christ was born of a virgin. Both were called "sons of God" (Luke 1:35; 3:38). Christ is the second Adam—a term mentioned by Paul in Romans 5:14 and 1 Corinthians 15:22 and 45.

In Genesis 14, the first king-priest was Melchizedek, a ruler in the early city of Jerusalem (called Salem in Genesis 14:18). Melchizedek was also a type of Christ, as he served both as king and priest, even as Christ is the ever-interceding High Priest in heaven and will return to earth as king of Kings. He is a priest after the Melchizedek order (Heb.5:5-10; 7:1-17).

Certain places and nations in the Bible can also be identified with types that are later revealed in the Scripture. Egypt represents the world system and spiritual bondage, which includes your spiritual condition before your conversion (Gal. 4:3; Rom. 6:17). Jerusalem or Zion typifies the heavenly Mount Zion and heavenly Jerusalem (Gal.

4:25-26; Heb. 12:22; Rev. 21:2). Babylon in the Old Testament was the headquarters of an Empire that took the Jews captive for seventy years. However, in the Apocalypse, Babylon represents an apostate church system (Rev. 11:8; 14:8; 17:5).

Various types continue in the Scripture. The Old Testament Tabernacle of Moses and the Temple of Solomon was divided into three sections or chambers: the outer court, inner court, and Holy of Holies. These three chambers are a type of the tri-part being of man, who is the temple of the Holy Spirit, as well as a body, soul and spirit (1 Cor. 3:16; 1 Thess. 5:23). The water from the flinty rock and the manna that fell six days a week in the wilderness are a type of Christ, who is the bread from heaven and the living water (Jn. 6:32; 1 Cor. 10:4). In the wilderness, the brass serpent on the pole typified Christ's death on the cross, as He bore our sins in His body on the tree (Num. 21:8; John 3:14).

As you can see, an entire book could be written on how Christ, the church, and events in the future were concealed in types, shadows. and patterns.

DISCOVERING PROPHETIC LAYERS

The term prophetic *layer* is not a theological term, as most theologians and scholars interpret the Scripture using the original language, word for word and verse by verse, to announce their interpretations. However, in the Hebraic mind, the Scripture holds different layers of possible interpretation. There is the *simple meaning* of the verse or story, or the plain sense of the text. You can read it and know what it says without asking any questions. For example, Joseph was in Egypt, went to prison, and later rose to power. That is the narrative (see Gen. 37-42).

However, in the story of Joseph are practical applications, such as how to hold on to your dreams; how not to compromise in a situation; and how God's favor will raise you up. Most ministers have applied the story of Joseph with similar applications, such as teaching others how to trust God when negative circumstances are ruling your life. This concept of application is a second layer of the story called the *practical application principle.* Most Biblical stories conceal some form of a practical application for our lives today.

Then there is *prophetic imagery,* such as that of Joseph mirroring the suffering Messiah, which causes rabbis to identify a future suffering Messiah as Messiah, son of Joseph. One of the great prophetic layers is found in Genesis 22, when Abraham traveled with his son Isaac for three days to offer Isaac upon an altar at Mount Moriah. The details of this event were penned by Moses, while the similar narrative was later repeated when Christ became the anti-type, fulfilling the type.

Following are the parallels between Abraham and Isaac, and Christ on Mount Moriah (see Genesis 22:1-14):

Abraham and Isaac	The New Testament Anti-Type
Occurred on Mount Moriah in Jerusalem	Christ was crucified on Mount Moriah in Jerusalem
Abraham was the father of Isaac	God is the Father of Christ
Isaac was the covenant son	Christ was the only begotten Son of God
Two unnamed men were there	Two unnamed men crucified on Golgotha
Abraham saw the mount on the 3rd day	Jesus was raised from the grave on the 3rd day
Isaac was laid upon the wood	Christ was laid upon the wooden cross
Isaac got up off the altar	Christ arose from the grave
A ram replaced Isaac	Christ was sacrificed in our place
A "lamb would be seen"	Christ is the "Lamb of God" who was seen

A prophetic layer is uncovered when we see that people, events, or holy days have within them the imagery of prophetic events that are to occur in the future. These layers are not always understood until the future event begins to unfold and the prophecies are being fulfilled. Such is the case with the seven feasts of Israel. The seven feasts of

Israel can be thought of as *decoder keys* that reveal the timing and the fascinating patterns that will unfold in future events.

Christian theologians traditionally do not use rabbinical methods of interpreting Scriptures. Teachers generally compare Scripture with Scripture, and ministers often compare the original Hebrew, Greek, and Aramaic words with other textual words to glean a clarification on the specific meaning of the word or passage. The deeper meanings, such as mentioned above, are discovered as the layers are peeled away to expose the hidden types, shadows, and patterns.

As an example, the Sabbath (called Shabbat) was established by God at early creation, when after six days of creative work, God rested on the seventh day (Gen. 2:2). Every seventh day was set aside as a Sabbath of rest for the people of Israel and was perpetual from generation to generation (Exod. 20:10-11). Note that God's creative work was completed in six days and that, in God's sight, one day with the Lord is as a thousand years, and a thousand years is as one day (2 Pet. 3:8). Using this concept, some of the early fathers and even certain rabbis considered it possible that the government of man will endure for six thousand years (six prophetic days). The seventh day will be a day of rest, with the Messiah ruling on earth for one thousand years (Rev. 20:4).

Israel's calendar was based upon the cycles of the moon and not the sun. The Hebrew word for month is *codesh*, a word used to identify the new moon which began each Hebrew month. The moon experiences four cycles each month: from full to half and from half to dark, then from dark to half and from half to full. It takes slightly over fourteen days for the moon to progress from darkness to fullness, and another fourteen days from fullness to darkness. Then we see the new moon.

The prophetic layer concealed in this fact is that Israel began in darkness and obscurity with Abraham, and fourteen generations later Solomon built a magnificent Temple, expanding the kingdom to its historical heights of wealth and power. Beginning with Solomon to the Babylonian captivity, Israel moved from full light of blessing to total spiritual darkness of apostasy, finding themselves held captive in Babylon, an enemy nation. Thus one *prophetic layer* found within the moon's monthly cycle is that the cycle reveals the prophetic spiritual cycles of Israel.

THE SEVEN APPOINTED TIMES

God spoke to Moses during Israel's wilderness journey and established seven major feasts, which are called *moedim*, or "appointed times." Seasons were marked and celebrated each year, and were to be perpetual from generation to generation.

> *"And the LORD spoke to Moses, saying, "Speak to the children of Israel, and say to them: 'The feasts of the LORD, which you shall proclaim to be holy convocations, these are My feasts."*
> - LEVITICUS 23:1-2 (NKJV)

The feast is an appointment or fixed time. We think of a feast as a huge banquet where everyone is eating until they cannot eat another bite. However, during one of Israel's seven feasts, Yom Kippur, also known as the Day of Atonement, the people fasted instead of feasted.

These feasts were also called a *convocation*; the Hebrew word being *mikraw* (Lev. 23:3, 7, 8), which means a *public meeting or a rehearsal*. Being a rehearsal, it was intended to be a preview of something in the future. In Leviticus 23:6 the Hebrew word for feast is *chag*, which is the root word for *chagah*, meaning to *move in a circle or to dance*. From these words we glean the understanding that these feasts were a called and appointed public convocation, a time to rejoice in the Lord, and yet a preview of events to come. Each of these seven feasts also initiated a season of rest and refraining from work as the celebration began (Lev. 23:7, 8, 21, 25, 35-36).

The following chart gives the English and Hebrew names of each of the seven major Biblical feasts, along with the month the feast is set on the Jewish calendar:

English Name	Hebrew	Month or Time of the Festival
Passover	Pesach	1st month the 14th day
Unleavened	Hag HaMatzah	1st month the 15th – 21st
First Fruits	Bikurim	1st Sabbath after Passover

Pentecost	Shavout	50 days from First fruits
Trumpets	Yom Teruah	7th month the 1st day
Atonement	Yom Kippur	7th month the 10th day
Tabernacles	Sukkot	7th month the 15th day

If we take the set month on the Jewish calendar and give the equivalent month on our secular calendar, we can identify the set months in which the seven feasts are to be celebrated and remembered:

English Name	Jewish Month	English Equivalent
Passover	1st month the 14th day	March/April
Unleavened	1st month the 15th–21st days	March/April
First Fruits	1st Sabbath of Unleavened Bread	March/April
Pentecost	50 days from First Fruits	May/June
Trumpets	7th month the 1st day	September/October
Atonement	7th month the 10th day	September/October
Tabernacles	7th month the 15th–21st days	September/October

These feasts are set times, meaning they are to be marked on the same days during the same Hebrew months each year. Since the Hebrew calendar centers on the moon cycles, this makes a lunar year an average of 354 days instead of 365 solar days, causing an average difference of eleven days between the lunar and solar calendars. Left untouched, this difference of eleven days each year would eventually cause the spring feasts to shift from spring to summer and the fall feasts to slide into the winter months, completely throwing off the intended harvest and rain cycles that were to run parallel with the spring and fall feasts. Thus the Jews add an additional month, seven times in nineteen years, to keep the feasts on their proper schedule.

Below is a chart revealing the Jewish month, the season of the year, and the set feasts identified with their proper date:

Hebrew Month	Seasons of the Year	Special Season
Nissan	March or April	The season of Passover
Iyar	April or May	The counting of the Omer
Sivan	May or June	The season of Pentecost

Tammuz	June of July	A fast on the 17th of the month
Av	July or August	Tishah B'a
Elul	August or September	The season of Repentance
Tishrei	September or October	Trumpets, Day of Atonement, and Tabernacles
Mar Cheshvan	October or November	Known as Cheshvan
Kislev	November or December	The season of Hanukkah
Tevet	December or January	A fast on the 10th day
Shevat	January or February	T Bishvat (New Year for Trees)
Adar	February or March	The feast of Esther and Purim holiday
Adar II	Added occasionally	To keep the feast days in their proper seasons

These set feasts were celebrated each year for one day, or up to seven days. These feasts have a practical, spiritual, and prophetic application. The practical application is they are centered on Israel's seasons of harvest and rain.

The three main harvests in ancient Israel are barley, wheat, and grapes (or the fruit trees such as figs, pomegranates, and olives). The three spring feasts of Passover, Unleavened Bread, and First Fruits center around the barley harvest. The early summer feast, called Feast of Weeks (Pentecost), centers around the wheat harvest. Early fall feasts—Trumpets, Atonement, and Tabernacles—were timed with the grape harvest and ingathering of the fruits of the land. As for rain, Israel's rain cycles begin in the late fall and extend through the early spring, and are known as the early and the latter rains (Joel 2:23; James 5:7).

SPIRITUAL APPLICATIONS

The spiritual application is clear. The seven festivals are all linked to major events surrounding Israel's departure from Egypt, their journey in the wilderness, and their entrance into the Promised Land. The Passover commemorated the blood of the lamb that was struck on the three outer posts of the doors of the Hebrew homes, which supernaturally protected Israel's firstborn sons from death (Exod. 12:7-14). Unleavened Bread was to remind the people that when they departed, they did not have time to place leaven in their bread during their journey as they had to depart quickly; and during the accrual feast, no leaven was permitted in the house for seven days (Exod. 12:15-20). The third spring feast called First Fruits was to mark the first ripened barley in the land and to introduce the ritual of presenting a sheaf to the Lord at the Temple for forty-nine days (Exod. 23:16-19).

Pentecost was called the Feasts of Weeks (Exod. 34:22), and was the celebration linked to the wheat harvest. It also commemorated God giving the Law to Moses on Mount Sinai. The three fall feasts of the blowing of trumpets were a memorial (Lev. 23:24). Yom Kippur, called the Day of Atonement, was designated as one day out of the year when atonement would be made on behalf of the Israelites, the Levites, and the High Priest. This was done by the High Priest himself, who entered the Holy of Holies on the tenth day of the seventh month (Lev. 16). The final (seventh) Torah Feast was Tabernacles, which commemorates the Hebrews spending forty years dwelling in tents in the wilderness. The people were to dwell in special man-made booths during the entire seven days (Lev. 23:39-43).

Most Biblical teachers acknowledge and understand the above information, as these instructions for the feasts are written in Exodus and Leviticus. However, some have failed to point out the astounding prophetic applications that are concealed, not only in the spring feasts, but also in the fall feasts. These provide a preview of prophetic events yet to be fulfilled. Before we explore the details and unveil numerous prophetic layers, it is important to understand the meaning of a special Biblical number—the number seven.

THE PROPHETIC MEANING OF THE NUMBER SEVEN

There are seven major Torah Feasts. The word seven is mentioned 463 times in the English translation of the Bible, and the word seventh is found 120 times. This number is considered a sacred number that is often linked to spiritual and other important events. The Biblical meaning of the number seven is *completion, perfection* or *a conclusion*.

The number seven is first mentioned in the story of creation, where God rested on the seventh day (Gen. 2:2) after completing six days of His plan for creation:

- **The first day** – God made light (Gen. 1:3)

- **The second day** – God divided the firmament (Gen. 1:7)

- **The third day** – God gathered the waters together – seeds and herbs (Gen. 1:10-11)

- **The fourth day** – God created the sun, moon and the stars, lesser and greater light (Gen.1:14)

- **The fifth day** – God created the fish and the fowl (Gen. 1:20)

- **The sixth day** – God created man (Gen.1:26)

- **The seventh day** – God rested (Gen. 2:2)

God is not a man that He can tell a lie (Num. 23:19); neither is He weary, nor does He faint (Isa. 40:28). God neither sleeps nor slumbers (Ps. 121:4). With these facts in mind, why would God require rest on the seventh day? I have often said that God rested since there was nothing else for Him to create! Also, the concept of resting on the seventh day was to establish a *pattern* for all of mankind to set aside a day of rest during the week to repose from their labors. As slaves in Egypt, the Hebrew people worked non-stop building treasure cities for Pharaoh. After departing from Egypt, God instructed them that both they and their animals were to cease from labor every seventh day (Exod. 23:12).

The seventh day was especially sanctioned and sanctified (set apart) by the Lord with a special blessing:

> *"And God blessed the seventh day, and sanctified it: because that in it he had rested from all his work which God created and made."*
>
> – GENESIS 2:3

In Biblical numbers, the meaning of the number is often discovered in the law of first mention; meaning, find the place in Scripture where the number is first used, and its application in that passage sets the pattern for its meaning throughout the Bible. As an example, man was created on the sixth day, and the number six throughout the Bible is linked to mankind. In the Apocalypse, the number of the beast (anti-christ) is six hundred, sixty and six, and is called the number of a man (Rev. 13:18).

Throughout the Torah, the number seven becomes linked with rest, freedom, release, and completion. From the time of creation, through the days of Moses, and into the revelation of the Apocalypse, the number seven is spiritually significant and God Himself begins initiating events in cycles of seven. The number seven begins in Genesis chapter 2 and continues through the book of Revelation!

We know that every seventh day was a day of rest; however, God later established a sabbatical year, meaning that every seventh year should be set aside to allow the people and even the land to rest:

> *"But in the seventh year shall be a sabbath of rest unto the land, a sabbath for the LORD: thou shalt neither sow thy field, nor prune thy vineyard."*

> - LEVITICUS 25:4

There is a practical purpose for this instruction. When the same crops are continually planted and harvested, the minerals in the topsoil will eventually be depleted, thus diluting the mineral levels in the food that is grown. However, when the land is allowed to lay fallow and the produce is not harvested, the food can fall to the ground on the seventh year and replenish the soil with nutrients.

After revealing the Sabbath week and the sabbatical seven-year cycle, the Almighty established a third sabbatical cycle which was a season of *Jubilee release*. During the Jubilee, in which the people were to count seven cycles of seven sabbatical years, they blew the silver trumpets on the forty-ninth year on the Day of Atonement to announce the year of Jubilee. Every fiftieth year a Jubilee was announced.

This word Jubilee is the Hebrew word *yovel*, which is used for the blast of a horn, such as a trumpet or a shofar. In this case it alludes to the blasting of the silver trumpets introducing the festival of Jubilee. Leviticus 25:8-9 reads:

> *"And thou shalt number seven Sabbaths of years unto thee, seven times seven years; and the space of the seven Sabbaths of years shall be unto thee forty and nine years.*
>
> *Then shalt thou cause the trumpet of the jubilee to sound on the tenth day of the seventh month, in the Day of Atonement shall ye make the trumpet sound throughout all your land."*

Hundreds of years after the death of Moses, the Jews were taken into captivity for seventy years (Jer. 25:11). This number is prophetically unique as it can be derived from a combination of the number *ten* multiplied *seven* times. In the Torah, God gave ten main commandments for Israel to follow (Exod. 20). However, He warned them that if they disobeyed Him, they would be punished seven times (Lev. 26:18). After inheriting the Promised Land, Israel broke all ten of those commandments, and God punished them seven times for each commandment broken; thus ten multiplied seven times gives us the seventy years of punishment in Babylon.

Daniel was in Babylon reading the scroll of Jeremiah and seeking God about the time of Israel's release and return from their captivity (Dan. 9:2). The angel of the Lord revealed to Daniel that another prophetic cycle was assigned for Israel, called the *70 weeks prophecy*. This indicated a 490-year timeframe divided into three parts. The final part is identified as seven years, and is marked by prophetic scholars as being the first reference in the Bible to the future seven-year great tribulation in which the antichrist will set up a dangerous eighth empire on earth (Rev. 17:11-12*). Thus, the number seven is linked directly to God and His prophetic purposes in the earth.*

THE NUMBER SEVEN IN THE MINISTRY OF JESUS

The significance of the number seven is also found throughout the life and ministry of Christ, especially in His redemptive sufferings. Christ was crucified on the eve of Passover and the suffering Messiah (son of Joseph) shed His blood on seven different parts of His body:

1. His head	crown of thorns	- John 19:2
2. His back	the beating	- Matthew 27:26
3. His left hand	a nail	- Luke 24:39
4. His right hand	a nail	- Luke 24:39
5. His left foot	a nail	- Luke 24:39
6. His right foot	a nail	- Luke 24:39
7. His side	a spear	- John 19:34

Not only did Christ shed His blood on seven places on His body, but He also spoke seven distinct sayings from the cross:

"Father forgive them, they know not what they do."	- Luke 23:34
"Today you shall be with me in paradise."	- Luke 23:43
"Woman, behold your son; behold your mother."	- John 19:26-27
"I thirst."	- John 19:28
"Father, why hast thou forsaken me?"	- Mark 15:34
"Father, into your hands I commit my spirit."	- Luke 23:46
"It is finished."	- John 19:30

There were also at least seven major witnesses on earth at the moment of the crucifixion:

1. The religious leaders	- Luke 23:50
2. The Roman centurion	- Matt. 27:54
3. The Roman soldiers	- John 19:23
4. The Jewish women	- John 19:25
5. The Disciple John	- John 19:26
6. The two thieves	- John 19:18
7. The spectators	- John 19:20

Christ also descended at the seventh hour of His crucifixion into the heart of the earth. Mark 15:25 indicates that Christ was on the cross at the third hour, which would have been nine o'clock in the morning. Luke 23:44-46 reveals that Christ cried out, "Father, into your hands

I commit my spirit" at the ninth hour, which would have been three o'clock in the afternoon. Christ was on the cross for six hours, but at the beginning of the *seventh hour* of suffering, He died and His spirit descended into the lower parts of the earth (Eph. 4:9-10).

BACK TO THE FUTURE

According to Daniel 9:27, there is a future seven-year-cycle which, when concluded, will end with the return of Christ to earth to rule and reign from Jerusalem for a thousand years (Rev. 20:4). These seven years are divided in the middle with two sets of forty-two months, or each set being 1,260 days each (Rev. 11:3; 12:6).

Prophetically these seven years are identified as the tribulation, in which the future antichrist will form a final kingdom. Great judgments and distress will be upon the earth for a total of seven years. This time is referred to by Jeremiah as the time of "Jacob's trouble" (Jer. 30:7).

From a rabbinical perspective, Jacob's trouble alludes to the time when Jacob was working for his uncle Laban in Syria, and worked seven straight years to gain the hand of marriage from Laban's daughter, Rachel. Instead, he was given the oldest daughter Leah. Laban told Jacob that if he desired to marry Rachel, he must "fulfill her week" (Gen. 29:27-28). Jacob worked an additional seven years *(notice the word week here was a week of seven years and not seven days)*, to marry the woman of his dreams. He didn't just work seven years; he actually worked a total of *fourteen years* for one woman! This was known as Jacob's trouble. Thus, of the twenty years spent in Syria (Gen. 31:38), Jacob's time of trouble was two periods of seven years each. This event can hold a special prophetic layer of understanding.

When Christians teach a future seven-year tribulation, calling it Jacob's trouble, many Jewish rabbis will point out their opinion that Israel's time of trouble has already occurred in the past, during the time of the terrible holocaust. From around 1938 to 1945, Hitler set out to persecute and annihilate the Jews, arresting them en masse, sending them to concentration and death camps, and murdering about six million Jews, including a million and a half children. This tragic time for the Jews spans seven years. Thus, to some in the religious Jewish community, Jacob's trouble is not a future event but a past nightmare in Israel's history.

However, there is a prophetic layer found within these two periods of seven years: one period of seven might have been fulfilled during the holocaust, while the other seven years will be fulfilled during the future great tribulation.

At the conclusion of the first seven years of tribulation known as the holocaust, Israel was rebirthed as a nation in 1948. There is another seven years linked with the antichrist who, as Hitler did, will attempt to annihilate the Jewish people. At the conclusion of the final seven years of tribulation, Israel's eyes will be opened to receive Christ as Messiah, bringing Israel to salvation. These two layers can also be found through the meanings of the names of the sons of both Leah and Rachel, these two wives of Jacob.

After marriage, Rachel was barren, but Leah had four sons. Leah's firstborn was Reuben, and when he was born, Leah confessed that *the Lord has seen my affliction* (Gen. 29:32). Her second son was Simeon and she said, *The Lord heard my cry...I was hated* (Gen. 29:33). Her third son was Levi and she predicted, *"I will be joined with my husband"* (Gen. 29:34). After the birth of her fourth son Judah, Leah rejoiced saying, *"I will praise the Lord"* (Gen. 29:35).

If we consider the seven-year holocaust and the meaning of the names of Leah's sons, we can sum up the meaning of their names in one sentence: *The Lord saw (their) affliction, heard their cry, and joined them back to their land where the area of Judah was reestablished.* God did see the affliction and suffering of the Jews, and He did hear their cry. He joined them back to their original land after the holocaust, and Israel was re-established as a nation in 1948.

If Jacob's seven years with Leah contain a code of Israel's restoration after the holocaust, then Rachel's seven years represent the future seven years. This would mean that Rachel's sons should have names that hold some prophetic meaning for the final seven years.

Rachel's handmaiden gave birth to several sons, but Rachel gave birth to only two sons, Joseph and Benjamin. When Rachel was dying as she gave birth to her second son Benjamin, she named the infant Ben-oni, which in Hebrew means "son of sorrow." But Jacob changed the newborn child's name to Benjamin, the "son of the right hand" (Gen. 35:18).

In the narrative we see that Rachel has *one son with two names*: the first name refers to the sorrow and pain of the childbirth, while the new name means the "son of the right hand." During the seven-year tribulation, Israel will experience what is termed the "birth pains of the Messiah." They will experience a time of great sorrow—a time known by the prophets as travail (Isa. 66:8). Christ called the season the beginning of the birth pains (Matt. 24:8). However, out of the pain, suffering and travail of the tribulation will come forth the Messiah—the son of the heavenly Father's right hand (Heb. 1:3)—known as Christ Jesus who will deliver Israel from her enemies of destruction.

SEVEN CHURCHES AND SEVEN BLESSINGS

The beginning of the book of Revelation addresses seven churches that existed in Asia Minor in John's day. The Lord gave each church a special and distinct promise of blessing if they remained faithful.

The Church	The Blessing Promised	The Link to the Seven Feasts
Smyrna	Not hurt by the second death	Passover
Pergamos	The hidden manna	Unleavened Bread
Philadelphia	New name, a pillar in the Temple	First Fruits
Thyatira	Power over nations, rule with rod of iron	Pentecost
Laodecia	Sit on my throne	Trumpets
Sardis	White stone; will not blot out of book	Atonement
Ephesus	Eat of the tree of life	Tabernacles

Astonishingly, these promises given to the seven churches each hold a clue that is linked to a specific aspect of the one of Israel's seven feasts. Smyrna is not hurt by the second death, which is parallel to the Passover blood of the lamb that prevented death from entering the house of the Hebrews (see Exod. 12). Pergamos, if they repent, was promised the hidden manna, which links with Israel's second feast, Unleavened Bread. Just as the manna was specially prepared bread from heaven, Israel's second feast involves special bread that is made without leaven in the dough.

The church of Philadelphia was told that they would be given a new name and made a pillar in the house of God. This is a picture of the third feast of Israel—First Fruits. During First Fruits, the new and first grain is offered to the Lord at the Temple. Thyatira, if they overcome, was promised power over the nations, to rule them with a rod of iron. During Pentecost (Acts 2:1-4), Jews were gathered out of all the nations and are seen in the Temple. Through the power of the Holy Spirit, God gave the church the authority to take the Gospel to the nations and proclaim His name and kingdom (Acts 2:1-8; Mark 16:15).

The Laodicean church was promised that, if they overcame, they could sit upon the throne of Christ. Traditionally, the Feast of Trumpets is viewed by devout Jews and rabbis as the feast honoring the coronation of the King or the wedding of the King—thus the King upon His throne.

Sardis, if they repent and strengthen what remains, would be given a white stone and their name would not to be blotted out of the Book of Life. This imagery is found in Israel's sixth feast, the Day of Atonement. It is on this day that a heavenly decision is made to either blot out or retain the name of a person in the Book of Life in heaven.

Finally, Ephesus was told that if they overcome, they could eat of the tree of life. The seventh Feast of Tabernacles is linked to trees, as there are four types of trees, including certain trees with branches that are used to form the outdoor canopy called a sukkot or a booth.

THREE SIGNIFICANT FEASTS

The three main feasts occurred during three different seasons: spring, summer and fall. Of the seven feasts, all males over age twenty had to attend three of them each year in Jerusalem:

> *"Three times you shall keep a feast to Me in the year: You shall keep the Feast of Unleavened Bread (you shall eat unleavened bread seven days, as I commanded you, at the time appointed in the month of Abib, for in it you came out of Egypt; none shall appear before Me empty); and the Feast of Harvest, the firstfruits of your labors which you have sown in the field; and the Feast of Ingathering at the end of the year, when you have gathered in the fruit of your labors from the field. Three times in the year all your males shall appear before the Lord GOD."*
> -Exodus 23:14-17 (NKJV)

The first feast was Passover, the second Pentecost, and the third was Tabernacles—the first, fourth and seventh feasts. Why were these three selected from among the seven? Herein is another prophetic layer.

Passover originated in *Egypt,* Pentecost was established when Israel was in the *wilderness,* and Tabernacles was to be celebrated after Israel entered the *Promised Land.* Notice the order of progression. Egypt was a territory controlled by *Satan's domain*; the wilderness represents the *world's domain* with numerous obstacles to overcome; and the Promised Land is *God's dominion.* As believers we are delivered from the bondage of Satan (Egypt), and begin our journey that takes us through the dangers of life (the wilderness), until our journey ends in the Promised Land, where we enter into our rest.

In Egypt, slavery is a theme. In the wilderness, being servants of God is the primary focus. In the Promised Land, being a son of God is necessary to inherit all spiritual blessings. We have moved from slaves to sin, to servants of God, and on to the level of sons (and daughters).

There is a further prophetic layer concealed in these three feasts. When dealing with Satan's territory (Egypt), the blood of the lamb must be applied to prevent the destroyer from entering your house. The Hebrews placed the blood of the Passover lamb on the outer door posts and ate the lamb in their house (Exod. 12). The blood brought protection from death, and eating the body of the lamb provided physical healing for Israel before their long journey. In like manner, Christ the Lamb of God shed His blood, and today we overcome Satan by the blood of the Lamb and by the word of our testimony (Rev. 12:11).

His blood brings us freedom from the bondages of Egypt—a picture of the land of bondages of Pharaoh and Satan.

Pentecost, or the Feast of Weeks, was birthed in the wilderness when Moses received the commandments from God. The emphasis of the Pentecost harvest is wheat, which is a perfect picture of the bread of God's Word, and how that God provided heavenly bread for His people during their entire journey in the wilderness (and through our lives). The wilderness was full of danger, including bitter water (representing bitterness), fiery serpents (representing fiery trials), and seasons of testing and even times of unbelief. However, supernatural provision with manna, water from a rock, and shoes that never wore out sustained the nation during forty years.

Christ taught that we should pray, "Give us this day our daily bread" (Matt. 6:11). We are also informed that we cannot live by bread alone, but only by every word that comes from the mouth of God. As wheat was a food staple for the Hebrews, Pentecost is the time when the living bread, Jesus Christ, must be given to the nations.

Once Israel entered the Promised Land, they lived in homes they did not build, and ate from vines they did not prune and fruit trees they did not plant (Deut. 6:10-11). They came into their inheritance. Six foods of Egypt are listed in the Bible: fish, cucumbers, melons, leeks, onions, and garlic (Num. 11:5), but there were seven foods in the Promised Land: wheat, barley, grapes, figs, olives, honey, and pomegranates (Deut. 8:9). Spiritual fruit will mature in the life of a person who comes into the fullness of their relationship with God—or their spiritual Promised Land.

The death of Christ near Passover would impact the Jews, because during the public condemnation of Christ before Pilate, the religious Jews placed a blood curse upon themselves and their children (Matt. 27:25).

On the day of Pentecost, the Holy Spirit-filled believers were all in one place in the upper room, early in the morning during the Feast of Pentecost (Acts 2:1-4).

The Feast of Tabernacles is a picture of the coming kingdom, in which all nations of the earth will go up to Jerusalem to worship during this annual feast (Zech. 14:16-19).

THE SPIRITUAL APPLICATION

The people attending these three feasts also present a dynamic spiritual application for the life of a believer. Passover is the season of your redemption, when you enter into a redemptive covenant with Christ. Pentecost is the season representing your baptism in the Holy Spirit, and Tabernacles can be an imagery of the resurrection of your mortal body and your entrance into the millennial kingdom of the Messiah.

The application of all being present is that no one can stand in your place to receive redemption for you, as a salvation covenant is an individual act of faith. You alone must ask in order to receive, as it is written, "With the heart one believes unto righteousness and with the mouth confession is made unto salvation" (Rom. 10:10). You must be present when the blood is applied to the doorpost of your heart at Passover.

Since the Holy Spirit was promised and poured out at Pentecost (Luke 24:49; Acts 1:8), the second feast all men were required to attend reveals the second blessing after your redemptive covenant. That is the promise of the gift of the Holy Spirit. In the upper room they were "all filled" (Acts 2:4), indicating that at Pentecost no person was left out of the outpouring. Salvation is personally received and the Holy Spirit is also a gift for those individuals who ask and believe (Luke 11:13). Each man was present at Pentecost and you must be present when the Holy Spirit is flowing to receive your spiritual blessings.

Feast of Tabernacles is unique and, as you will discover later, there are many facets to this wonderful week of convocation and rejoicing. All men, including Jews and Gentiles, participated in this season of joy and all males over twenty traveled to Jerusalem for this final feast. In the wilderness, the people lived in tents; but God Himself also dwelt in a portable tent called the tabernacle. When the tabernacle was rolled up and transported, the priest would first remove the sacred furniture, then take down the skin coverings, then separate the boards. The resetting of the tabernacle was in a reverse order, which is a beautiful picture of the resurrection. The boards were set up first, then the skins covered the boards, and the sacred furniture was then set inside of the skin tabernacle. This is a picture of a Believer who is raised from the dust in a new resurrected body.

Only the Almighty could have laid out such a remarkable pattern, thousands of years before the occurrence of the actual event that He had concealed within the pattern.

Mankind's adversary, Satan, no doubt observed God's appointed seasons because, over time, he set out to disrupt the appointments God made with His people. Why did Satan choose these seasons? We will delve into this in the next chapter.

CHAPTER 2

SATAN'S DISRUPTION OF GOD'S APPOINTED SEASONS

O VER 3,500 YEARS ago, one of the greatest transfers of people from one nation to another occurred. On the morning after the first Passover, six hundred thousand men of war, along with their wives and children, loaded their possessions and headed toward the Red Sea—a massive body of water that must, somehow, be crossed to enter the Sinai desert. Just when they thought the king of Egypt was defeated, they heard the rumbling of chariots behind them, accompanied by rolling clouds of dust.

The adversary would attempt to pin Israel between land and sea, and crush them at the edge of the sea. But God opened the waters and Israel crossed on dry land. When the enemy attempted to cross, the walls of water closed upon them and Pharaoh met his death in the briny deep.

Passover was the night the death angel passed; Unleavened Bread was the following day when Israel departed; and the death of Pharaoh and his army fell on the day that would later become the week of First Fruits. The entire conflict with Egypt and the evil Pharaoh, and Israel's victory in the wilderness, was accomplished within one week.

Now, move ahead slightly over forty years to the fortified city of Jericho where, prior to the conquest, Joshua circumcised the men and celebrated Passover. The Israelites were then told to march around the city for six days and to shout on the seventh (Josh. 6:3-10). The crossing of Jordan, the circumcision of the men, and the encircling of Jericho all align with the spring feasts of Israel. Notice how the order of events in Joshua chapters four and five fall in line with the spring feasts:

Hebrew Date	Main Event	Timeframe of the Feasts
10th of Nissan	Joshua initiated circumcision of the men	four days before Passover
14th of Nissan	Joshua kept the Passover with Israel	the Feast of Passover
15th of Nissan	Joshua and the people ate the grain of the land	the Feast of Unleavened Bread
16th of Nissan	Joshua initiated the six days of marching	the Feast of First Fruits

RAHAB—THE FIRST FRUITS MOTHER

Before Israel crossed the Jordan the river was flooding, which indicated that the spring rains were falling. This would have been around the time of the barley harvest (Josh 3:15). Jericho was the first of over thirty Canaanite cities that Israel would conquer (Joshua 12), and the conquest of this city began during the Festival of First Fruits. This timing initiated the commandment that all of the possessions of Jericho were to be sanctified and set apart as a First Fruits offering to God and His Tabernacle:

> *"But all the silver and gold, and vessels of bronze and iron, are consecrated to the LORD; they shall come into the treasury of the LORD."*
> – JOSH. 6:19 (NKJV)

This is why God required that all of the possessions from the city be consecrated for the treasury of the Tabernacle. In the Law of First Fruits, if the first fruit is offered to God and is blessed, then the remaining produce in the field will be blessed. By offering Jericho as a First Fruit offering to God, or the first conquered city, God ensured that Israel would be successful in conquering the remaining Canaanite cities.

On the seventh day, or near the conclusion of First Fruits, the walls fell. But miraculously, God spared Rahab, the harlot who hid the two spies and lived in a house on the wall, as well as her entire family (Josh. 2:5; 6:22). In Israel today, tourists can see clay bricks and even bits of charred wood from the different time periods of the ancient city of Jericho.

Here is an interesting fact. Jericho was a *first fruits city* and Rahab was the *first convert* to the true God from among the inhabitants of Canaan. Her faith is mentioned by Paul in Hebrews 11:30-31 (NKJV):

> *"By faith the walls of Jericho fell down after they were encircled for seven days. By faith the harlot Rahab did not perish with those who did not believe, when she had received the spies with peace."*

She is also mentioned in James 2:25 (NKJV):

> *"Likewise, was not Rahab the harlot also justified by works when she received the messengers and sent them out another way?"*

As the first convert, the Law of First Fruits placed a special blessing on the future harvest, once the first fruits were presented to the Lord. Rahab was the town harlot, but was justified by faith due to her action in protecting the two spies and sending them out safely, and by believing that the God of the Israelites was the true God. How did God place a special blessing in Rahab's future?

The Gospel of Matthew provides a list of forty-two individuals in the genealogical tree of Jesus, from Abraham (Matt. 1:1-17) to Christ Himself. Women are seldom mentioned in ancient genealogies, as the emphasis is placed upon the name of the father and his son, since the family name is passed to the next generation through the son. Matthew, however, lists five women in the family tree of Christ: Thamar (1:3); Ruth (1:5); the wife of Uriah (1:6); Mary (1:18); and Rahab (1:5). We read:

> *"Salmon begot Boaz by Rahab, Boaz begot Obed by Ruth, Obed begot Jesse, and Jesse begot David the king."*
>
> – Matthew 1:4-6 (NKJV)

After Rahab's house was spared from the rubble of Jericho, she married a man named Salmon from the tribe of Judah. Rahab conceived a Biblically well-known son named Boaz. This is the same Boaz who married the Moabite widow named Ruth, whose story is recorded in the book of Ruth.

The fields of Boaz were in Bethlehem, the leading city of the day in the tribal land given to Judah. Moving forward three generations from Boaz, the Biblical genealogies indicate that David was born in Bethlehem. We learn that Rahab was the mother of Boaz, the great-grandmother of Jesse, and the great-great-grandmother of David! Her decision to convert to Israel's God at the conclusion of the Hebrew season of First Fruits released the first fruits blessing on her entire future. The linage of the House of David was given the promise to bring forth the Messiah who would rule from David's throne in Jerusalem forever (2 Chron. 21:7; Zech. 12:10).

Rahab's story is one of victory during First Fruits. However, there is another well-known Jericho narrative that did not turn out so well. Jericho was set apart as the *first* of numerous Canaanite cities to be conquered by the Hebrews in the days of Joshua. As stated, Jericho's possessions were consecrated for the Lord's House and were not to be personally kept as spoil of war. Joshua placed a verbal curse upon anyone who would personally withhold any possessions from the city (Josh. 6:18). One man named Achan, from the tribe of Judah, went into the city, secretly seized garments, gold, and silver, and hid them in his tent. He believed no one would discover his actions, or he certainly would have thought twice before sinning.

ACHAN: THE FIRST FRUITS CURSE

Joshua said, *"Keep yourselves from the accursed thing, lest ye make yourselves accursed"* (Josh. 6:18). The Hebrew word *accursed* is *herem*, which can refer to a devoted thing or a consecrated thing. In modern Judaism the Hebrew the word *herem* is a ban that is imposed on an individual to separate him from the other members of the community. The possessions of Jericho were consecrated to God; but if an Israelite chose to disobey and steal the spoil, then the consecrated things would become a cursed thing and the individuals would be separated from the community and severely punished.

Joshua and the Israelites decimated Jericho, and then prepared to invade a smaller city named Ai. The Hebrew troops were overconfident, sending only three thousand men to the city. During the battle, thirty-seven of Israel's soldiers were slain and the men of Ai chased the remaining 2,963 Hebrew soldiers away from the walls of their city.

Joshua fell on his face complaining to God for withdrawing His promise to defeat their enemies. The Lord rebuked Joshua, telling him that one of his men possessed accursed spoil from Jericho. Achan was exposed, stoned, and his body burned to prevent further failure in battle (see Joshua 7-8).

When the spoils of the city were marked as first fruits and presented to the treasury of God, the favor of God rested upon the remaining efforts of Joshua to capture the other cities. However, when the first fruits were withheld, then a curse followed upon those withholding what belonged to God. This spiritual principle is emphasized in Malachi, when the prophet wrote concerning the giving of tithes and offerings:

> *"Will a man rob God? Yet you have robbed Me! But you say, 'In what way have we robbed You?' In tithes and offerings. You are cursed with a curse, for you have robbed Me, Even this whole nation. Bring all the tithes into the storehouse, That there may be food in My house, And try Me now in this, Says the LORD of hosts, If I will not open for you the windows of heaven And pour out for you such blessing That there will not be room enough to receive it."*
>
> - MALACHI 3:8-10 (NKJV)

Obedience opens windows and disobedience closes windows. The adversary used the sin of Achan during the season of the Feast of First Fruits to bring God's disfavor, causing a serious setback in Israel's battle strategy. Throughout the history of Israel, Christ's ministry, and the time of the early church, one of Satan's strategies was to initiate an assault during God's appointed seasons.

Several years ago I was studying the various attacks that came against Christ in the four gospels, and I observed the timeframe linked with persecution against the early Christians. Many of the adversary's strongest attacks and attempts at opposition occurred during one of the feasts. The following list illustrates this:

Appointed Seasons	Reference	The Attack that Transpired
Feast of Passover	John 5:1	The Jews sought to slay Jesus
Feast of Passover	John 6:4	A life-threatening storm struck the boat on the Galilee
Feast of Passover	John 11:55	The Pharisees sought to take Him
Feast of Tabernacles	John 7:11	The Jews sought Jesus out at the feast
Feast of Dedication	John 10	They sought to stone Him
Feast of Unleavened Bread	Luke 22:1-3	Satan entered Judas's heart
Feast of Passover	Matt. 26:2	Christ was arrested and taken to trial
Feast of Pentecost	Acts 2:1-4	Persecution immediately followed the Spirit's outpouring
Feast of Pentecost	Acts 20:16	Paul was arrested in Jerusalem

What would be the significance of the adversary agitating the enemies of Christ during significant feasts days? After researching the question, I believe there are four specific reasons why attacks were planned against Christ and the disciples to coincide with the appointed seasons of God.

1. THE LARGEST CROWDS WERE PRESENT

Each time Christ celebrated Passover in Jerusalem, it seemed that some secret plot to remove Him from public ministry was organized. Each time it failed, until the Passover of the crucifixion. Josephus wrote a brief commentary on the Passover of AD 66 in Jerusalem, and he said that at least ten men, and as many as twenty, were present at each sacrifice. He reported that 256,500 lambs were offered. If his numbers are correct (some scholars believe they are too high) this would imply that over two million people attended Passover in Jerusalem (*Josephus*, War 6.9.3. 422-427). Others estimate the numbers of attendees at 300,000 to 500,000.

Whatever the actual count, the fact that all men over age twenty were required to attend three feasts meant that men from every tribe, and many Jews from other nations, traveled to Jerusalem for this major, yearly festival. Such massive crowds provided the haters of Christ and the religious hypocrites with a platform to spread rumors faster than a wildfire on a prairie, thus energizing and uniting their power base to generate negative publicity against Christ. The more controversy created, the more doubt created toward Christ's ministry. The plan was to plant hateful and negative words among the multitude when the largest numbers of people were present.

2. HIS GREATEST OPPOSITION WAS IN THE CROWD

The majority of Christ's ministry took place in the upper and lower Galilee region, where most of Christ's disciples lived and worked. Galilee was known in Hebrew as "Galilee of the Gentiles" (Isa. 9:1), and the region was a trade area for Gentiles traveling the roads connecting the lower Galilee to Jordan, Syria, and Lebanon.

The religious center and center of the nation was Jerusalem, the headquarters for the Pharisees, Sadducees, Doctors of the Law, and scribes. The common people in Galilee gladly received Christ. However, most of Christ's adversaries and critics lived in and around Jerusalem and were His chief opposition during Passover, Pentecost, and Tabernacles. Thus, during these Jerusalem feasts, more of Christ's enemies were in attendance than at any other city in Israel. So Christ's opposition was stronger and their numbers larger in Jerusalem during the three main feasts.

3. SATAN KNEW GOD HAD MARKED EVENTS ON FEASTS

No doubt the adversary had observed events and celebrations during these appointed seasons throughout Israel's long history and understood these days were special to God. Any spiritual observer also noted that major prophetic events seemed to coincide around the feasts.

Many scholars believe that Christ was conceived at or near the time of Hanukkah, the yearly Jewish celebration of lights which often falls in December on our calendar. This would have meant Christ's birth would occur nine months later, most likely during one of the fall feasts—perhaps Tabernacles. It is pointed out that the shepherds were watching their sheep by night in the fields (Luke 2:8), whereas in a cold winter sheep would have been placed in caves during the night, where fires would be lit to keep the shepherds warm. Mary laid the infant in a manger, which is a feeding trough for animals, carved from limestone and usually placed near a stable where animals are kept at night.

Have you wondered why someone in the local inn did not give up a room for this pregnant woman who was about to give birth? (Luke 2:7). If Christ was born during the week of the Feast of Tabernacles, it is possible Mary gave birth under a sukkot, or one of the many outdoor booths that would have been constructed onto the houses in the area. This Tabernacles theme is cryptically alluded to in John 1:14, where it is written that the Word (Christ) was "made flesh and dwelt among us." The word *dwelt* in Greek is *skenoo*, which means to tent or to encamp. Assuming Christ was born near the beginning of Tabernacles, the Law required that He be circumcised on the eighth day, which would have fallen near the eighth day of Tabernacles, the day recognized as "the rejoicing in the Torah" (Luke 2:21). When Mary and Joseph brought Jesus to the Temple, Simeon and Anna were "rejoicing" in the Messiah (Luke 2:25-28).

Using Christ's fall birth as a pattern, the baptism and temptation of Christ become more significant when considering the possible feast link of these noted events. Christ was baptized when He was about thirty years of age (Luke 3:23), the same designated age of a male priest when he was appointed to Temple service (see Num. 4).

If we use the first day of Tabernacles for the birth, then Christ also would have been baptized in the Jordan during the fall feasts season. The Feast of Tabernacles was to commemorate Israel's forty years of dwelling in tents in the wilderness. When Christ came up out of the water of the Jordan River, He immediately traveled to the heart of the Judean wilderness (just a short distance from Jordan) where He was tempted during a forty-day period (Matt. 4:2). Dwelling in the wilderness for forty days is parallel to Israel's wanderings in the wilderness for forty years (Neh. 9:21), where Israel was also tempted. Israel failed in their temptation, but Christ overcame during His temptation! Satan himself was present during the entire forty days to tempt Christ. According to this chronology, Satan targeted Christ during the fall feast season.

4. SATAN WAS ATTEMPTING TO KILL CHRIST BEFORE THE TIME

After the birth of Christ, Herod ordered Roman soldiers to slay all infants under the age of two who lived in or around Bethlehem. Jerusalem was only six miles from Bethlehem and the cries of the mothers whose infants were slain was heard from Bethlehem through Ramah, which was a city in the tribal region of Benjamin (Jer. 31:15; Matt. 2:18). Rachel was the mother of Benjamin, and while giving birth to him, she died and was buried near the entrance to Bethlehem (Gen. 35:18-20). Jacob gave Benjamin his name, meaning "son of my right hand." Both Benjamin and Judah shared the tribal land grant near the edge of the Temple in Jerusalem.

Herod was informed that the future king of the Jews had been born in Bethlehem, thus he chose to slay all infants under age two, just to be certain he also killed the infant king. However, Ramah was in the land of Benjamin, and Jeremiah predicted a voice of weeping would be heard in Benjamin.

There may be two important insights into the Ramah prediction. First, the people of Judah and Benjamin were very close, and when word came of the deaths of the infants, weeping was heard in both Judah (Bethlehem) and Ramah (the area of the Benjamites). Herod knew the prophecy of the Messiah's birth in Bethlehem (Mic. 5:2; Matt. 2:5-6), and those around him knew that Benjamin was the "son of the right hand." Could Herod have expanded his death sentence into the land of Benjamin to prevent the infant king, who might have been hiding in the area of the Benjamites, from ever coming forth as the "son of God's right hand?" This "post-birth abortion process" by Herod was the earliest attempt to kill Christ before He could mature into manhood.

At age thirty, during the temptation cycle, Satan brought Christ to Jerusalem at the pinnacle of the Temple and told Him to jump and see if angels would prevent Him from being physically harmed (Matt. 4:6-7). This would have been suicide, as this pinnacle was about seven hundred feet high! According to Josephus, anyone standing on top of the wall and looking down at the Kidron Valley would become dizzy.

After His temptation, Christ traveled to His hometown of Nazareth where His first sermons provoked the townspeople into grabbing Him and leading Him to the edge of a cliff to throw Him off (Luke 4:28-30). Jesus wouldn't jump seven hundred feet at the demand of Satan; so now the enemy could mock Him, as Christ would be forced to fall from a high place! However, He escaped and found safety in the lower Galilee.

Later we read of another attempt, this time to drown Christ in a boat when a sudden storm struck and the boat filled with water. He exercised authority over the storm and brought peace to a troubling situation (Mark 4:37-41). On another occasion, Christ traveled to Jerusalem where a remnant of His enemies made an attempt to stone Him at the Temple. They "sought to kill Him" (John 10:31).

All of these above battles were designed to kill Christ prematurely, but all of Satan's assignments failed.

MODERN ISRAEL AND YOM KIPPUR

Even the modern enemies of Israel at times take advantage of Israel's seasons of fasting and prayer by initiating surprise wars and attacks against the Jewish state. One well-known war was Israel's fourth war with surrounding Arab nations in 1973 on the Day of Atonement, today known as the Yom Kippur War. It was fought from October 6–25, when a coalition of nations led by Egypt and Syria made a surprise attack on the Jewish state. On Yom Kippur, devout Jews spent the entire day fasting and praying in the synagogues. Israel was unprepared for the swift and undetected movements of the Egyptian and Syrian forces. The motivation for the war was for Egypt and Syria to regain all of the territory lost in the Six-Day War of 1967.

Arab armies attacked in Israel's seasons of fasting and rest. After not eating, a soldier would become physically weak. This plan to "attack when they are hungry" is also the strategy of Satan when he tempted Christ after He had fasted forty days. Luke 4:1-3 tells us that after Christ hungered, the tempter came and commanded Him to turn stones into bread.

Traditionally, Israel seldom, if ever initiates a war during any of the major feasts, as this season is considered sacred and holy and the nation is filled with tourists. However, the enemies of Israel, just like your spiritual enemy, have no respect for holy things or for the things of God. Christ recognized this when He said to Peter, *"Get behind Me, Satan! You are an offense to Me, for you are not mindful of the things of God, but the things of men"* (Matt. 16:23 – NKJV).

CONSIDER YOUR OWN BLESSINGS AND ATTACKS

As a Believer, you also experience attacks around certain cycles, times, and seasons. As indicated in this book, Passover represents the blood of the Lamb (Christ) who provides for your redemption. The feast of Pentecost represents the baptism of the Holy Spirit, while the Feast of Tabernacles is a preview of the promise of the resurrection from the dead. The adversary will attempt to prevent you from entering a redemptive covenant by keeping you under the spiritual bondage of Pharaoh (Satan).

Once you have been born again (John 3:3) by experiencing your Passover redemption, the next blessing is fulfilled with the Holy Spirit. To some this is a challenge, because voices will arise to discourage Believers from pursuing a personal Pentecost and encountering the Holy Spirit with the evidence of a prayer language (Acts 2:4). Some churches have Passover without Pentecost, or salvation with no emphasis on the baptism in the Spirit. However, Pentecost is one of the three major feasts that all men are required to attend.

Once a Believer has experienced their Pentecost through baptism in the Spirit, they must move into understanding their prophetic future in the kingdom—the picture of Tabernacles.

Your spiritual attacks might not necessarily fall in line with the Jewish holidays, but as a Believer you will have your seasons and cycles of testing and temptation. These movements of the adversary are targeted for important life cycles and seasons in your life. When Satan stopped tempting Jesus, Luke wrote that Satan departed from Christ "for a season" (Luke 4:13). The Greek word season is *kairos*, and it refers to a set or appointed time, which figuratively means a more opportune time. This "more opportune time" usually strikes you when you are physically, emotionally, or spiritually weak.

I began to understand how these cycles work when I first started to list the unusual cycles of blessings and attacks within my own family. I first observed that there is a unique twenty-year age difference between many in the family—between my Grandmother Bava and my mother; between my mother and my older sister; between my older and younger sisters; and between my younger sister and my nephew.

Below are some interesting patterns that emerged in our family:

- My mother had a miscarriage at the same age that my wife had a miscarriage.

- Dad and I were the same age when each of our wives had the miscarriage.

- Both my mother and my wife Pam had a little girl after their miscarriages.

- Pam and my mother were the same age when their girls, Melanie and Amanda were born.

- My brother Phillip was twelve when his sister Melanie was born; our son Jonathan was twelve when his sister Amanda was born.

- My mother and my brother were the same age (28) when they had gallbladder surgery

- My dad, grandfather, and I were the same age (17) when we began evangelizing.

- Granddad began his church in June of 1959—the same week I was born.

- I preached my first sermon in Dad's church and my first revival in Granddad's church.

- My brother has an older son and a little girl; we have an older son and a little girl.

- My son Jonathan was filled with the Spirit exactly 25 years to the night I preached my first revival in Maryland.

These unusual cycles that repeat themselves were observed by Solomon, as he wrote in Ecclesiastes 1:9-10 (NKJV):

> *"That which has been is what will be, That which is done is what will be done, And there is nothing new under the sun. Is there anything of which it may be said, "See, this is new"?*

OTHER SPECIAL SEASONS

Other interesting celebrations were marked for specific seasons. Israel had a new wine festival which arrived seven weeks—or about fifty days—after Pentecost. According to the Temple scroll (columns 19-21), nobody was permitted to drink of the fresh fruit of the vine until the new wine was offered at a ceremony at the Temple. On the day of Pentecost, the disciples were accused of drinking new wine (Acts 2:13), which was technically impossible as it was not the season. Then there was a New Olive Festival that was celebrated fourteen weeks after Pentecost and just before the Feast of Trumpets. Nobody would begin to crush the new olives in their own vineyard until the first new olives had been offered at the Temple. The majority of the olive harvest came after the Fall Feasts.

The outpouring of the Holy Spirit is the oil and wine being poured upon the Believers. The Bible often uses metaphors to speak in a figurative language. Grapes are made into wine, and the new wine represents the fresh outpouring of the Holy Spirit that produces the joy of the Lord. Olives are essential to making oil, and the oil of anointing is a picture of the anointing of the Holy Spirit that flows over a person, just as natural oil flows from the head to the feet when poured upon the head.

THE PROPHETIC IMAGERY

Ancient Israel enjoyed the grain, grape, and olive harvests. The grains of barley and wheat were crushed to make bread, the grapes crushed for wine, and the olives crushed to bring out the golden oil. Just as the first grain harvest is barley, the prophetic Scriptures identify a "first fruits ingathering" of men, identified as the 144,000 Jews from the twelve tribes who are called the first fruits of the tribulation harvest (Rev. 14:4).

The grape harvest is also referred to in Revelation 14:18-19, when an angel takes his sickle and thrusts it into the grape vines and throws the cluster into the wine press of God's wrath.

I believe the olive harvest is represented by the Jewish remnant that survives the global shaking during the great tribulation. While this great tribulation is sweeping the globe, both Old and New Testament saints, along with Jews and Gentiles from the church age, will be in heaven rejoicing with the Lamb.

The ultimate goal of your spiritual enemy is to disrupt the plan of God for your life and interfere with God's appointed seasons. When I was born, for two weeks I was unable to hold down any milk or baby formula. I began losing weight until they found a formula I could drink. At age two and a half, I was in a serious automobile accident that could have cost me my life. Other accidents occurred during my lifetime, including being in a private plane that lost an engine in flight. In my earlier ministry, I could have married a certain young girl and missed God's will by not marrying Pam, my true sweetheart and life's mate.

On one occasion in a church in New York, I was preparing to pray in the basement in the pastor's office when I spotted a large knife in the pastor's chair thrust through holding a death note. I ran from the church and immediately the police were informed. The pastor's briefcase was found in a boiler room, and it was later believed the culprit was hiding in the large closet behind the air units, across from the pastor's office.

We have all experienced close calls in life, and only the Lord knows how many times angels have been assigned to protect us by slapping a roadblock on the trail of the slithering serpent to prevent him from crossing a forbidden line into our lives.

After decades of ministry, I have concluded that many physical, spiritual, and emotional attacks on Believers are based upon a *threat assessment* from the adversary. However, it is important to understand that God has set a particular destiny for each person, known in simple terms as, "the will of God." Think about the Apostle Paul and the numerous times his life was in danger:

- Acts 9:24-25 - Jews attempted to kill him, but he escaped in a basket over the wall.

- Acts 14:19-20 - He was stoned in the city of Lystra and left for dead.

- Acts 23:12 - While imprisoned in a castle he spoke, and Jews took an oath to kill him.

- Acts 25:3 - In Jerusalem, the religious Jews were lying in wait to kill him.

- Acts 27:42 - A major shipwreck could have drowned him, but he swam to an island.

- Acts 28:3 - He was bitten by a poisonous viper and should have died, but he didn't.

Every assault against Paul was defeated, although he was beaten five times with stripes and three times with rods and bore on his body the literal marks and scars from being physically abused for preaching Christ (2 Cor. 11:24; Gal. 6:17). The adversaries of the gospel were unable to stop him, as he wrote:

> *"But the Lord stood with me and strengthened me, so that the message might be preached fully through me, and that all the Gentiles might hear. Also I was delivered out of the mouth of the lion. And the Lord will deliver me from every evil work and preserve me for His heavenly kingdom. To Him be glory forever and ever. Amen!"*
>
> *– 2 TIM. 4:17-18 (NKJV)*

During Paul's ministry, the adversary plotted a premature departure for Paul; however, destiny prevailed and Paul fulfilled his assigned mission. When the time came for Paul's death, he wrote:

> *"For I am already being poured out as a drink offering, and the time of my departure is at hand. I have fought the good fight, I have finished the race, I have kept the faith."*
>
> *– 2 TIM. 4:6-7 (NKJV)*

Paul did not depart until his assignment was complete and he was ready to be poured out as a drink offering.

SHE DIDN'T JUMP OUT THE WINDOW

I heard an older women share a touching story of her life years ago, when she was living in an apartment in Chicago. Her husband worked in the city and they had one small child. The woman became pregnant again and was battling depression. One day the enemy spoke into her mind, telling her that she should take her life. All she needed to do was jump out of the apartment window and meet her death when she struck the ground.

As she contemplated this temptation to commit suicide, suddenly she heard a still small voice say, "Why don't you give your child life?" She struggled to regain control of her thoughts, but knew God was speaking to her and telling her not to take her life and that of the infant in her womb. She did not commit suicide, and she gave birth to a beautiful daughter. Eighteen years later, her daughter became my wife, Pam Stone. Thank the Lord that her mother heard the voice of life and not death, and destiny prevailed.

The adversary assigns his many spirit rebels (Eph. 6:12) to attempt to destroy God-given destinies and generations. Today, youth around the world are experiencing attacks such as suicide, addictions to drugs and alcohol, depression, fear, and sexual confusion. Perhaps his strategy is similar to the plots against Christ: destroy Him before He can fulfill His prophetic destiny. The sons and daughters in the final generation are marked for a specific blessing and outpouring of the Spirit. We cannot sit back and allow them to be threatened by the adversary.

The only way we can effectively defeat the forces of darkness in our own lives and the lives of our family members is to bring the presence of God into our lives and our homes. This can be accomplished only by making ourselves available to the Holy Spirit and encountering His presence. Too many Believers, instead of approaching God's presence, are found hiding from the Lord when He shows up—just as ancient Israel did at Mount Sinai. We will explore the reasons for this in the next chapter.

CHAPTER 3

HIDING AFAR OFF
AT PENTECOST

THE FIRST "PENTECOST" was the giving of the Law to Moses on Mount Sinai, which initiated God's laws and instruction penned in the Torah. The first five books of the Bible include the world's early history; the exodus of the Israelites from Egypt; the building of the Tabernacle in the wilderness; the ceremonial, sacrificial and judicial applications of the Law; and specific instructions to follow once Israel entered the Promised Land.

One would think that the Hebrew nation, after four hundred years of living in Egypt, would enjoy their freedom and express sincere worship to God who redeemed them from Pharaoh. However, when any group of Believers consistently rubs shoulders with heathen idol worshippers, as generations pass, the truth of God's Word can become corrupted as pure truth is mingled with idolatrous beliefs. Israel's greatest challenge might have been that there was no specific, written Word of God, as there were no written commandments and laws of the Almighty for about 2,500 years, from the time of Adam to the time of Moses on Mount Sinai. Every person tended to do what was right in his own eyes (Judg. 17:6; 21:25).

The Hebrew people had mixed with the Egyptian culture prior to coming out of Egypt, as was evident when, within fifty days after their departure, the former slaves were dancing around a golden calf that had been formed by Moses's brother, Aaron. One of the false deities among the Egyptians at that time was a bull god named Apis that was worshipped and recognized as the god of prosperity and agriculture.

The reasoning among the Hebrews must have been that, since there was no food in the wilderness, they must seek a god that allegedly could provide for them during their journey. The people were out of Egypt, but the thinking of Egypt was not yet out of their minds.

Contrast how Moses and the people perceived the presence of God. Moses knew God face to face (Exod. 33:11). But the people knew God only by the miracles of the plagues, the exodus, and the crossing of the Red Sea. The Bible says that God made known His ways to Moses and His acts to the children of Israel (Ps. 103:7). The Hebrew word ways refers to the mode of action or the proper path taken, while the word acts is the performance, exploits, and actions of God. The people served God for what they saw, but Moses for what he knew. Put another way, the people knew about God; but Moses knew God personally.

THE FEAR OF GOD'S PRESENCE

The children of Israel are very much like many contemporary Believers in the average church today. Israel was familiar with three specific spiritual blessings by the time they reached Mount Sinai. First, they understood the message of redemption through the blood of the lamb. Over 3,500 year later, the Body of Christ understands that the foundational message upon which the New Covenant is based is redemption through the blood of the Lamb of God, Jesus Christ (Rev. 12:11).

Israel also understood that God is a healer, because after eating the body of the lamb, God brought health to their bodies. The church has understood that communion, or the Lord's Supper, is the process of receiving the fruit of the vine and the bread in remembrance of the blood and body of Christ, whose blood brings redemption, and whose body brings healing. There are various forms of healing, including physical, spiritual and emotional, which impact the body, soul and spirit of Believers.

The third truth that Israel knew and the church understands is the message of prosperity, as we read that, "God brought Israel forth with plenty of gold and silver, and not a feeble person was among their tribes" (Ps. 105:37). The gold and silver would later become the offerings of the people given for the building of the Tabernacle.

As with Israel, the power of redemption through the Lamb's blood, communion, and prosperity are three messages a Believer generally understands in the average contemporary Western congregation. But something began to shift among the ancient Israelites as the people advanced from redemption in Egypt to Mount Sinai.

As Moses prepared to ascend the mountain to meet face to face with God, the people of Israel requested that Moses speak to God on their behalf, as they did not wish to approach Him directly. The people camped at the base of the mountain, remaining at a safe distance from God, as Moses moved closer toward the Divine Presence on the Mount. They were also fearful because they saw the top of the mountain burning with fire (Exod. 20:18-21). Oddly, the people were familiar with the manifestations of God while in Egypt, yet when the thunder, lightning and fire descended upon the top of Sinai, they became afraid. Instead of worshipping God, they stood afar off.

Contemporary Christians remind me of ancient Israel anytime there is a demonstration of the Spirit of God. They settle into a comfort zone when the spiritual teaching or doctrinal instructions are not challenging. But when a message challenges their thinking, or when real worship breaks out, and praise becomes holy noise as the atmosphere shifts and is charged with the thunder and fire of God, they resist and attempt to hide from God's presence. I have watched people walk out of a church service, simply because the presence of God was moving from the heavenly Temple to the congregation, and they feared that the Spirit of the Lord would dislodge them from their comfort zone.

In Israel's case, while Moses was on the Mount with God, the people decided to change their manner of worship. Instead of worshipping the invisible God, they constructed a visible, man-made golden calf. Then they danced around it. Since this cow was an image of an old traditional Egyptian idol, we might say that the Hebrew children were steeped in the religious traditions of the Egyptians, and they exalted man-made ideas about religion above the true revelation of

God. The Egyptians worshipped many gods, and Israel lived under this culture for hundreds of years. So Israel built a sacred cow and exalted Egyptian tradition above Hebrew truth.

HIDING AT SINAI

The fact that the Hebrews were hiding at the base of Sinai conceals a message for Believers today. Throughout my entire ministry, I have taught on the infilling of the Holy Spirit, which is received as the act of the Baptism of the Spirit. I have personally witnessed tens of thousands of individuals receive the gift of the Holy Spirit (Acts 2:38). Over the years I have seen many church folks listen to clear teaching that explains the subject and answers many so-called controversial questions, yet these people still walk out the door and refuse to believe anything that goes against their traditions.

Why do we hide from God's presence? Israel hid from the presence of God because of their fear of the unknown. Adam, before his sin failure, personally met with God at the tree of life in the cool of the day when God would walk in the garden (Gen. 3:8). After he sinned by eating from the tree of the knowledge of good and evil, he hid from the presence of the Lord. The same voice that once thrilled him now frightened him (Gen. 3:8).

The difference was that, when Adam partook of the tree of life, he gained true relationship and knowledge of God; and true spiritual knowledge paves a path to walk in the Spirit! But when Adam ate of the tree of knowledge of good and evil, he gained carnal knowledge. We know this because Genesis 3:8 says that Adam knew he was naked and was ashamed. Individuals who are truly spiritual are drawn to the presence of God. Those who are carnally-minded will always flee in the opposite direction, because the carnal mind cannot receive the things of the Spirit of God (Rom. 8:7).

Adam sinned and disobeyed the command of God. The guilt of sin clashed with the holiness of God, thus convicting Adam and causing him to avoid his meeting place with God.

Why do people attend dry, dead and formal churches, when they could be sitting in a warm spiritual atmosphere of true worship and praise? I believe the common root is that they hide so not to be confronted with their own hidden sins or acts of disobedience. Israel became fearful when they witnessed God show up in the form of fire, thunder and lightning. Likewise, when certain manifestations—including speaking in tongues, words of wisdom, and words of knowledge—begin to flow in a congregation, some will move to the outskirts to avoid direct contact with the people in the midst of the outpouring.

When Moses was on Mount Sinai and the mount began shaking, this manifestation was a "new thing" for the Israelites, and this made them nervous. The parallel pattern can be seen today, as many reject any form of worship style, music, or spiritual manifestation they are unfamiliar with, even though all may be done in a Biblical manner and in spirit and truth. We stay with the routine, sing the songs we have sung for years, and know the order of service so well that we could sit at home with a clock and tell others exactly what is happening in the sanctuary at any moment.

On the first "Pentecost" on Mount Sinai, people reacted in a manner similar to those on the Day of Pentecost in Acts 2, when the Spirit was poured out! In Acts, when the Spirit came with cloven tongues as of fire and the disciples all began speaking in various known languages, some were amazed; some doubted; others questioned what it all meant; and others mocked (Acts 2:12-13). When church "as normal" moves from the natural to the supernatural, from form to fire, and from prose to purpose and power, some pew warmers will doubt, mock, or become skeptical. Others will, as some did on Pentecost, receive the blessing and step into a new spiritual dimension with God.

At Mount Sinai, God was within reach of the people, just as He is today. We can either choose to encounter His presence, or we can fearfully remain as far away as possible.

NO CONFIDENCE IN YOUR OWN PRAYERS

At Mount Sinai, the Hebrews wanted Moses to speak to God on their behalf. The parallel is that Believers often depend upon the prayers of others more than their own prayers. When Believers have some form of intense adversity, such as a sudden emergency or a severe sickness, the first response is to call a minister. They base this reaction on an admonition recorded in James, where he stated:

> *"Is anyone among you sick? Let him call for the elders of the church, and let them pray over him, anointing him with oil in the name of the Lord. And the prayer of faith will save the sick, and the Lord will raise him up..."*
>
> – James 5:14-15

What I often have seen, however, is that many Believers become so dependent upon the prayers of others that they have little confidence in their own prayer life. I know of a young man who had different struggles in his life, but believed in Jesus and the Bible. He was asked in a gathering to stand and pray, and was at first hesitant. He stated, "I'm really not sure if God hears my prayers." He was basing God's approval of him upon his spiritual condition at the time. My observation has been that many Believers would rather select someone they feel is closer to God than they are, and ask that person to approach God on their behalf. In their mind, this other person has more favor with the Lord, so surely their prayers are faster and more effective.

The Israelites at the base of Mount Sinai knew the spiritual condition of their hearts, and chose to view God afar off. They encouraged Moses to approach the Almighty to intercede and negotiate on their behalf. After all, they were in a barren, desolate wilderness and they needed food and water. When God did send manna, which was the food angels eat in heaven, the people complained:

> *"Now the mixed multitude who were among them yielded to intense craving; so the children of Israel also wept again and said: "Who will give us meat to eat? We remember the fish which we ate freely in Egypt, the cucumbers, the melons, the leeks, the onions, and the garlic; but now our whole being is dried up; there is nothing at all except this manna before our eyes!"*
>
> – Num. 11:4-6 (NKJV)

In Psalm 78:24, manna is called the bread from heaven and angel's food. Now, angels have existed in heaven much longer than men on earth, and clearly they eat food. Since manna is heavenly bread and angels have eaten it for thousands of years, how can several million Israelites complain after eating heavenly food? Yet they said the six foods of Egypt (earthly provision) were superior to the heavenly provision! Their problem was that the taste for the things of Egypt was stronger than their hunger for God and heavenly realities.

Israel was a nation of complainers. For forty years, they never ceased to verbalize negative opinions about things they did not like during their wilderness journey. The same is true in the Body of Christ today. Some of the most negative, pessimistic and sarcastic people in a community can be church members who complain about everything. The music is too loud, the preacher speaks too long, the air conditioner is too cold, the pews are too hard, they have to park too far away from the church, the youth are not dressed properly…and on the story goes. These individuals are often the ones who resist moving from the message of the blood of Passover to the power of Pentecost.

When I say Pentecost, I am not referring to a denomination or a particular religious sect of Believers. This word identifies an experience encountered by the early church when the Holy Spirit came upon them and they were all filled with the Spirit and began to speak with other tongues (Acts 2:4). This same Pentecostal experience is still valid, practiced, and available as a gift for Believers in our time (Acts 2:38-39).

At the time of Christ's trial and crucifixion, Peter followed Him afar off (Matt. 26:58), and many of the women beheld the scene of His suffering from afar (Matt. 27:55). When Believers begin serving Christ "afar off" and choose not to be closer because of fear of persecution or damage to our comfort zone, then we have settled at the base of the mountain.

Many individuals go only a certain distance in the realm of the Spirit, willfully choosing to allow others to climb up the hill in their pursuit of the Divine presence of God. Man's dwelling is always horizontal and God's presence is always vertical. Men without the Spirit, just as with ancient Israel, will dwell in dry places (the wilderness) and spend their years camped out in one place or wandering around in circles. Horizontal living requires little faith, as you live by sight and not by faith. Vertical living requires that a person look up, climb up, and move up from the low places to the heights of God's presence.

Paul said that we were made to sit together in heavenly places with Christ Jesus (Eph. 2:6). When you draw near to God, then God will draw near to you (James 4:8). At Passover, Christ was lifted up between heaven and earth to draw all men unto him (John 12:32). God's position of blessing is always to look up, as all good gifts come down from the Father in heaven (James 1:17).

The Pentecost of Acts 2 was the birth of the church on Mount Zion in Jerusalem. The blessing of Pentecost continues as Believers come out of the shadows of fear and tradition and make a vertical ascent into the presence of God!

CHAPTER 4

THE FEAST OF TRUMPETS
AND THE RAPTURE CODE

*"Therefore let us keep the feast, not with old leaven,
nor with the leaven of malice and wickedness, but
with the unleavened bread of sincerity and truth."*

– 1 CORINTHIANS 5:8 (NKJV)

THE THREE FALL feasts are the Feasts of Trumpets, the Day of Atonement, and the Feast of Tabernacles. These three feasts reveal a rich prophetic pattern for events that will transpire in the future. All three occur in the fall and all are on the same month—the seventh month on the Jewish religious calendar. In this section, I will explore the many prophetic insights concealed in the first of three fall festivals, called *Yom Teruah*, or the Feast of Trumpets.

The first fall feast occurs on the first day of the seventh month, the month of Tishrei. The name Yom Teruah means a *day of noise and blasts from the shofar*. The central feature of sounding the shofar gives this day its name, the Feast of Trumpets. This day is also known among the Jews as *Rosh Hashanah* or the *head of the year* which, on the Jewish secular calendar begins on Trumpets, the first day of the seventh month.

This day also begins a ten-day period called the Days of Awe leading up to the tenth day of Tishrei, the Day of Atonement. The purpose of the trumpets blasting is to wake up the people and prepare them for the coming season in which God is going to either judge them or justify them on the Day of Atonement. Among devout Jews, it is common to write a letter or greet a person with the words, "L'shana Tova," which is a wish for a good year, and to say, "May your name be inscribed in the book of life." These ten days are a reminder to repent and make oneself right with God. The Lord instructed Moses in Leviticus 23:24:

> *"Speak unto the children of Israel, saying, In the seventh month, in the first day of the month, shall ye have a Sabbath, a memorial of blowing of trumpets, an holy convocation."*

So we see that on the secular Jewish calendar, Trumpets—or Rosh Hashanah—is called the head of the year, and this begins the secular Jewish New Year on Tishrei the first. There is a Jewish tradition which indicates that Adam was created from the dirt on Mount Moriah in Jerusalem on this day. Twenty generations later, Abraham offered his son Isaac on the same mountain in Jerusalem, and this sacred hill became the same area where Christ was crucified and raised from the tomb.

The tradition of Adam's creation is based upon the first phrase of the Bible, "in the beginning," which is the Hebrew word *bereshit*. Rabbis change this to read *Alef b' Tishri*, which translates to the first of Tishrei. According to one Jewish tradition, Adam was formed on Rosh Hashanah and sinned against God on what would later be set as the Day of Atonement.

The central feature on the Feast of Trumpets is the number of trumpet blasts sounded. There are one hundred blasts of the shofar during this day. Interestingly, a gold-plated shofar and silver trumpets are used on this particular day. This is why the festival is also called "The Day of Sounding." Gold is a metal that represents *deity* and the *divine nature of God*, whereas silver is a precious metal representing *redemption*.

This day is also identified with many other names, including Yom Teruah, *the day of the awakening blast*, referring to the shofar sounded at the resurrection of the dead. Another theme identifies this day as

Yom Ha Din, referring to the Day of Judgment. As a side note, some rabbis suggest that there are twelve months in the year and Jacob's twelve sons were all born over time—one son on each of the twelve months. Since one of Jacob's sons is named Dan, which means, "God has judged," the belief is that he was born in the month of Tishrei, when God judges or remits the sins of His people.

Another term used to identify this day is Yom Zikkeron, which is the *Day of Remembrance*. Rabbis also call this day Ha Melech, the season of the *coronation of the King!* All of these themes—the awakening blast, the day of remembrance, and the coronation of the king—have prophetic allusions. The awakening blast occurs at the resurrection of the dead in Christ (1 Thess. 4:16-17). The day of remembrance is for those living at the time who make up God's jewels, and He will spare them from the tribulation (see Malachi 3:16-17). The coronation of the king could indicate that Christ returns and gathers together the Believers during the Feast of Trumpets, and returns to earth with the saints after the tribulation. There, in Jerusalem, He will receive coronation as the King of kings and Lord of lords (Zech. 14:9,16; Rev. 19:16).

Numerous prophetic teachers believe that the gathering together of the overcoming church, identified with the theological term "Rapture," will occur in the season of this feast. Both the gathering together and the resurrection of the dead in Christ will occur a few moments apart on the same day, at nearly the same moment of time. Paul wrote that the dead in Christ would rise (be resurrected) first, and then the living saints would immediately be changed from mortal to immortal, and rise from the earth to meet the resurrected Believers in the air (1 Cor. 15:51-52; 1 Thess. 4:16-17; Eph. 1:9-10).

The Feast of Trumpets, or Rosh Hashanah, is identified with the awakening blast of the trumpet. There will be at least two different blasts of the trumpets, since the resurrection of the dead and catching away of the living saints are two separate events happening moments apart. Paul wrote that the Lord would descend from heaven with the trump of God (1 Thess. 4:16). This trumpet blast will raise those who have died in Christ, and they will rise to meet Christ in the air. Paul also revealed that we who are living at the time will be changed at the sound of the last trumpet (1 Cor. 15:52). The first trumpet blast will raise the dead. A second blast will cause the living to be changed and caught up together with them in the clouds.

The first Biblical concept of the two trumpets is found in Numbers chapter 10. God instructed Moses to make two silver trumpets to be used for the calling of the assembly and the journeying of the camps (Num. 10:2). When *one* trumpet was blown, the princes of Israel gathered themselves together, and when *both sounded at once* the entire camp gathered at the door of the tabernacle. Certain types of blasts in various directions were signals for the people from that particular section to move forward toward the door of the tent. Another blast of the trumpet caused the people to go forward when making their journey.

When the time of Jubilee was established, these silver trumpets were used on the tenth day of the seventh month, which was also the Day of Atonement. Thus, freedom and liberty was declared every fiftieth year or Jubilee year, on the Day of Atonement. These Jubilee cycles would be a preview of Christ's death and resurrection, bringing the final atonement for mankind, and a jubilee of a lifetime of freedom from sin and Satan's dominion.

FOUR TYPES OF SOUNDS

On the Feast of Trumpets there are four significant sounds made from the shofar. The first sound is called *Tekiah*, which is one very long blast that sounds like an alarm. The second sound is *Shevarim*, which consists of three, one-second notes rising in tone. Then there is *Teruah*, which is nine quick, short blasts. The fourth is called *Tekiah HaGodolah*, which is the longest and loudest sound, in which the blower (called Baal Tekiah) blows air into the shofar until he runs out of breath. This usually lasts about ten seconds and is identified as the "last trumpet sound."

There are two schools of thought related to the trumpet of God and the gathering together of the saints, especially the "last trump." The first school of interpretation points out that Paul said the living would be changed at the "sound of the last trump" (1 Cor. 15:52), and in their belief, the last trump is the trumpet sounded by the seventh angel in the book of Revelation. They point out that this trumpet follows six other blasts of trumpets by six angels in a specific order, in which various earthly and cosmic judgments have been poured out. When the seventh angel sounds his trumpet from the heavenly Temple, they note that "the mystery of God is finished" (Rev. 10:7).

This is the last trumpet mentioned in the cannon of New Testament Scripture and the last time in the book of Revelation where the word trumpet is used. The word mystery is used in Revelation 10:7 and also used by Paul when he wrote, "Behold I show you a mystery." For these reasons, the assumption is that the coming of Christ for the Believer (the Rapture) will occur at some point during the middle half of the tribulation as the seventh angel sounds the seventh trumpet.

The second school of thought notes that the phrase "last trumpet" (1 Cor. 15:52) was written by Paul around AD 54. At times, Paul would write an epistle which, after being read in the churches, created questions that required Paul to follow up with answers in his second letter (such as 1 Thessalonians and 2 Thessalonians). Paul spoke of the last trump in his first letter, never giving an explanation to the readers of what he meant, nor giving further commentary in his second epistle to the Corinthian Believers. This is because the readers understood the Jewish concept of the "last trump," and they needed no further explanation. They knew that the last trump is the *Tekiah HaGodola*, the longest and loudest blast sounded when the final shofar sounds at the conclusion of the Feast of Trumpets.

The long and loud sounding of a shofar is found in the narrative where Moses ascends Mount Sinai in Exodus 19, which is also a perfect picture of the events surrounding the catching away and gathering together of the church to heaven. The following list illustrates the parallels:

THE SINAI REVELATION IS A PICTURE OF THE RETURN OF CHRIST FOR HIS CHURCH

Moses on Mount Sinai in Exodus 19	The Rapture and Second Coming
Israel was a peculiar people (Exod. 19:5)	The Church is a peculiar people (1 Pet. 2:9)
Israel was a kingdom of priests (Exod. 19:6)	The Church is kings and priests unto God (Rev. 1:6)
The people were to be sanctified (Exod. 19:10)	Believers are to sanctify themselves (1 Thess. 5:23)
God appeared on the third day (Exod.19:11)	He will raise us up on the third day (Hosea 6:1-3)
God came down in the clouds (Exod. 19:16)	He is coming in the clouds (Acts 1:9-10)
God came down in the lightning (Exod. 19:16)	He is coming as lightning (Matt. 24:27)
God's voice as a trumpet (Exod. 19:16)	The trump of God will sound (1 Thess. 4:16)
God answered Moses in a voice (19:19)	The voice of the archangel (1 Thess. 4:16)
God came down in fire (Exod.19:18)	Christ returns in flaming fire (2 Thess. 1:7-10)
God descended from heaven (Exod. 19:20)	Christ will descend from heaven (1 Thess. 4:17)
God called Moses up (Exod. 19:20)	The saints will be caught up (1 Thess. 4:17)

In Exodus 19, when the trumpet sounded loud and long, then the Lord came down and Moses went up! When the last trumpet sounds we shall be caught up to meet the Lord, who has descended from heaven, and we shall meet Him in the air.

For those who identify Paul's last trump with the trumpet of the seventh angel, note that the letter of 1 Corinthians was written around AD 54 and the book of Revelation was compiled around AD 96—over forty years later than the initial revelation of the last trump mentioned by Paul. There is no Biblical record of a Jewish believer asking Paul which last trump he was referring to, because the Jewish people were already familiar with the different blasts of the shofar. It was blown during the Sabbaths, the new moons, and feast days; therefore, they were aware that the last trump was linked to the final blasts on the Feast of Trumpets. There will be at least two major blasts of the shofar on the day Christ returns: one will raise the dead, and another will cause the living saints to be changed in a moment, in the twinkling of an eye (1 Cor. 15:52).

In Matthew 24, there is a first trump and last trump, referred to by Christ as the "great sound of a trumpet." Just as different trumpets are blown on various feasts, the various trumpet terms used in the New Testament can line up with various feasts. A trumpet is associated with Pentecost; the last trump with the Feast of Trumpets; and the great trump with the ingathering on the Feast of Tabernacles.

The last trump is also a great trumpet and will be blown twice during the seven-year tribulation. The first time occurs just prior to the beginning of the seven-year tribulation, at the catching away of the saints to heaven (1 Thess. 4:16-17). The second time occurs when Christ returns to earth to gather His Jewish elect who have been scattered to the four corners of the world (Matt. 24:31). Thus, we find a great trumpet at the beginning of the tribulation, and the second at the end of the tribulation. The details of Rosh Hashanah, or the Feast of Trumpets, encode many parallels of the anticipated catching away of the saints to heaven!

Since the blowing of shofars and trumpets is significant on this day, the theme of the resurrection and the gathering together of the saints fits the imagery perfectly. We read in Psalm 47:5, *"God has gone up with a shout, the LORD with the sound of a trumpet"*. The blowing of the shofar on Rosh Hashanah is referred to in Psalm 81:3-4, *"Blow the trumpet at the time of the New Moon, at the full moon, on our solemn feast day. For this is a statute for Israel, A law of the God of Jacob."* At the gathering together of the saints in 1 Thessalonians 4:16, the shofar blast is called the "trump of God." Then we are informed there is a sound of the "last trump" (1 Cor. 15:52). During the Feast of Trumpets, both gold and silver trumpets are used. Since gold represents deity, and since this trumpet is specifically identified as the "trump of God," it reasons that this imagery of blasting a gold trumpet would be a picture of the trump of God.

WHAT ABOUT THE DAY AND HOUR?

Christ gave a very important revelation to His followers regarding the day of His coming when He said:

> *"But of that day and that hour knoweth no man, no, not the angels which are in heaven, neither the Son, but the Father."*
>
> – MARK 13:32

One of the chief criticisms of someone who teaches that the gathering together of the church will occur on one of the major feasts, and specifically a fall feast such as Trumpets, is the above passage. If we suggest a particular feast day, then does this contradict the above verse? This apparent contradiction can be explained when we research certain Jewish details of the Feast of Trumpets.

Each month in Israel, the beginning of the month is announced with the visibility of the first tiny edge of the new moon (called Rosh Chodesh). To identify the beginning of the month, two witnesses were required to come to Jerusalem and meet in a courtyard called Beit-Ya'azek, where they rested and were fed until they were called to meet with the Great Sanhedrin. Once the testimony of the witnesses was confirmed, the Sanhedrin would face the inner court of the Temple and announce, "The day is hallowed;" and the people who gathered would reply, "The day is hallowed."

At that moment, a man on horseback would ride through the local villages to announce the day had begun. At the same time, a torch was lit from the top of the Mount of Anointing (the Mount of Olives). When the light was spotted on the other mountains, a torch was also lit from mountain to mountain, all the way from the mountains of Israel to Babylon and Persia, ensuring that the Jews living in all of those areas would know the feast had arrived.

Certain feasts, such as Passover, Unleavened Bread, and the beginning of First Fruits fell on the cycle of the full moon. Since the Feast of Trumpets was the first day of the seventh month, there was a *two day window in which no one knew the exact day or hour* when the blast of the first trumpet would occur.

Thus, this is the only feast of the seven in which *no one knew the exact day or hour* when the announcement of hallowing the day would be made. The prophetic parallel is clear. No one will know the exact day or hour of Christ's return, as the trumpets blasts are blown throughout the day, and no one is certain which part of the day or hour—or even which year—the return of the Messiah is planned.

Another rabbinical tradition points out that on Trumpets, the door of the heavenly realm is opened to the righteous. In the Apocalypse, after Christ addressed the seven churches (Rev. 2-3), John states that after he wrote to the seventh church, he saw a door in heaven open. A voice told him to come up, and immediately he was in the throne room of God in heaven (Rev. 4:1-2). This same pattern—the voice from heaven, the door opening, and the immediate transportation from earth to heaven—will occur simultaneously at the Rapture of the saints.

THE ARGUMENT AGAINST THIS OPINION

When Christ was revealed as the Lamb of God (John 1:29), He eventually fulfilled the three spring feasts, as Passover was themed around the blood of a lamb redeeming Israel from Egypt (see Exodus 12). Christ died on the cross prior to Passover (Matt. 26:2), was in the tomb as the sinless sacrifice for mankind during Unleavened Bread, and arose and showed Himself alive during the same time as First Fruits. Thus Christ fulfilled both the *chronological order* of the feasts and the *proper pattern* on the actual day or week of the feasts themselves.

One of the arguments from some Messianic believers is that it would be impossible to fulfill the chronological order of the three fall feasts. If the Rapture occurred on Trumpets, then ten days later arrives the Day of Atonement (representing the tribulation), and the future kingdom of the Messiah would come five days later after Atonement, since that is when Tabernacles begins. What might be overlooked is that the final seven-year tribulation is actually the missing 70th week of Daniel (from Daniel 9:27) and the prophecy of the seventy weeks (see Daniel 9). The last seven years completes a gap of prophetic time that ended the 69th week of Daniel at the crucifixion of Christ, and will initiate the beginning of the last week, or seventieth week, at the Rapture of the church and beginning of the tribulation. When the seven years is completed on earth, then the Messiah's visible kingdom is set up on earth and a thousand year reign begins (Rev. 20:4).

Thus, the chronological order of the major prophetic events, from the Rapture to the millennial kingdom, is found in the patterns concealed in the three fall feasts that parallel the prophetic predictions of both Old and New Testaments. The Rapture is the imagery of Trumpets, the tribulation is the imagery of the Day of Atonement, and the coming kingdom of the Messiah ruling on earth is concealed in the patterns of the Feast of Tabernacles.

Since the last Biblical feast to see a major prophetic fulfillment was Pentecost (Acts 2:1-4), the next feast in line to be prophetically fulfilled is the Feast of Trumpets. The next major event on the prophetic calendar is the resurrection of the dead in Christ and the catching away of the living saints to the heavenly Temple. Thus, the Rapture fits the time frame of this fall feast of Israel, or at least the pattern of the Feast of Trumpets.

OTHER CLUES IN THE FEASTS

Christ became our atonement, and the day of the crucifixion offers insight into the rituals of the Day of Atonement when we consider the two goats that were offered by the priest: one the scapegoat (the imagery of Barabbas) and the goat that died on the altar (a picture of Christ's crucifixion). By researching the Jewish history, oral traditions, and written rabbinical customs of the feasts, there are varied ceremonial processes that are parallel to future prophetic events.

An example is the priestly ordinances and practices at Passover. All of the lambs were not offered at once, but the rite was carried out in three shifts. The first offering was in the morning and was the most crowded. As soon as the courtyard was full, the gates of the Temple were closed and the services began with the Levitical choir singing. They were accompanied by musical instruments as they sang the Hallel—the Psalms of praise. When they finished the Hallel, there were three different blasts on silver trumpets—the *Tekiah, Teruah, Tekiah HaGodolah.*

Each worshipper provided a knife for the slaughter of the lamb. The priests were so fast and efficient that the choir only needed to sing the Hallel once. This process can be compared to the order in the book of Revelation. After these lambs were offered, the Temple Mount was cleared for the second group to arrive, where the same process was repeated. Finally a small group arrived for the third shift.

In Revelation chapters 2 -3, the seven churches are mentioned, and then John was told to write concerning the things that would be hereafter, or after the church age (Rev. 4:1). In chapters 4 – 5, the scene changes to the heavenly mountain where the door of heaven is seen opened and John arrived to a great multitude worshipping God in His sacred Temple.

In the parable of the ten virgins, the wise with oil enter the marriage supper and the door is shut behind them (Matt. 25:10), just as the gates of the Temple were closed to others during the first service. John heard a voice like a trumpet saying, "Come up here," and he was immediately caught up in the spirit from the Island of Patmos to the heavenly Temple.

Notice that silver trumpets were sounded at the Passover offering. In the Bible, silver represents redemption and the theme of Passover is redemption. Normally, ram's horns (called shofars) were blown in Israel at various seasons or times, and for specific purposes—such as a call to war. However, the silver trumpets were used during the Divine service; for announcing the Sabbath day, the New Moon, and the three main feasts; and during the Jubilee.

The main offering at Passover is the lamb, as each family brought one lamb for every ten men. When John was caught up into heaven, Christ, the Lamb of God, was introduced at the Temple as the Lamb that had been slain (Rev. 5:6), meaning the sacrifice was accomplished and completed. Christ's work was finished on the cross.

If this order is same as the earthy ritual, there must be singing in heaven, accompanied by instruments, when the slain Lamb is seen before God's throne. In Revelation 5:6 the Lamb is seen and in 5:8-12, the twenty-four elders take harps and sing a new song, "Worthy is the lamb that was slain who has redeemed us…" (Rev. 5:9). These first worshippers seen in heaven are the overcomers from the church who have been caught up and are gathering together in the heavenly Temple to worship God and celebrate the Lamb who has redeemed them.

Just as in the earthly Temple, a second group arrives at the heavenly Temple after the initial group, and this second group is seen in Revelation 7, where we read:

> *"After these things I looked, and behold, a great multitude which no one could number, of all nations, tribes, peoples, and tongues, standing before the throne and before the Lamb, clothed with white robes, with palm branches in their hands, and crying out with a loud voice, saying, "Salvation belongs to our God who sits on the throne, and to the Lamb."*
>
> – REV. 7:9-10 (NKJV)

John asked the angel who this multitude was, and the angel replied that they had come out of the great tribulation and made their robes white in the blood of the Lamb. Christ returned for the church in chapter four, for a group that was "without spot, wrinkle or blemish" (Eph. 5:27). The second multitude had "made their robes white in the blood of the Lamb" (Rev. 7:14).

I have heard Greek scholars, such as the now-deceased Dr. Ray Brubaker, point out that the tense used here implies that this multitude was spotted when the Rapture occurred, but had to make their robes white. Later they appear before the throne waving palms (an imagery of the Feast of Tabernacles), and singing a song to the Lamb—a song that is also sung by the first group.

If this Passover parallel is correct, there is a third group arriving after the second group has completed worshipping. This third multitude that is seen is recorded in Revelation 14, where the 144,000 Jews—twelve thousand from each tribe—are standing with the Lamb on the Holy Hill of God in heaven.

Notice that, in all three narratives, the Lamb is referred to as the Passover Lamb. This group also has harps and sings a new song, and these will follow the Lamb wherever He goes (Rev. 14:1-5). This group was first seen on earth, being sealed with a special protective seal of God, that prevented the judgments of God and the hand of the antichrist from reaching them (see Rev. 7). On earth these men had lived during part of the tribulation and are caught up sometime, either during or shortly after, the antichrist invades Jerusalem and sets up his headquarters. Thus, the rituals and imagery at the Passover, with the three separate divisions, can be seen in the book of Revelation with the church (Rev. 4), the tribulation saints (Rev. 7), and the 144,000 (Rev. 14).

COUNTING THE OMER

Between the festivals of Passover and Pentecost, there is a process called "counting the omer," and this also has significant prophetic implications. The word *omer* is used five times in Exodus 16, where manna fell in Israel's camp and the people gathered the white, heavenly bread each morning for food. The omer was actually a particular measure of a volume of grain; thus the manna was measured using the omer method.

During the spring harvest cycle, once the first grain of the barley harvest was offered to the Lord, the people were permitted to eat from their personal barley fields during the entire forty-nine-day counting of the omer. When Pentecost arrived on the fiftieth day, the offering and waving of two loaves of bread baked with wheat indicated the wheat harvest was ripe and the people of Israel could prepare wheat from their fields. In both the barley and wheat harvests, the first fruits must be offered to God before the remaining fields could be harvested.

Note that there is a first fruits, or first offering, of both barley and wheat presented at the Temple in Jerusalem; and after the ritual, the inhabitants of Israel were released to gather the cereal grains from their own fields. The prophetic principle here is that the first fruits of the harvest of souls must also be presented to God in His heavenly Temple before the main harvest of souls can be reaped on earth, as the field is the world (Matt. 13:38). The barley represents the Gentile church, and the wheat harvest is linked with the 144,000 Jews who are called the "first fruits of the Lamb" (Rev. 14:4).

Counting the omer was connected with the barley harvest. The commandment in the Torah was for the priests to make a daily count, from Passover to Pentecost, of forty-nine days; and each day, they were to take a sickle and cut an omer of ripened barley and present it at the Temple. This offering continued for forty-nine days, up until the day that the wheat offering was presented at the Temple on Pentecost. The count was made in days and then in weeks—or seven weeks of seven days. This is why Pentecost (a Greek word) is actually called the "Feast of Weeks" in the Torah (Exod. 34:22; Deut. 16:10). The omer count began on the second day of Passover, (the 16th of Nissan) and ended the day before Pentecost, which is the fiftieth day from the counting. The instruction is found in Leviticus 23:15-16:

> *"And you shall count for yourselves from the day after the Sabbath, from the day that you brought the sheaf of the wave offering: seven Sabbaths shall be completed. Count fifty days to the day after the seventh Sabbath; then you shall offer a new grain offering to the LORD."*

This counting was done to commemorate the preparation and the excitement of Israel receiving the Law, which was written on the stones by the finger of God Himself. Passover was Israel's redemption and Pentecost was the giving of Law.

GOD'S LAW OF COUNTING

In the Torah, on several occasions God instructed Israel to count certain things. First they counted the number of people in a family to ensure that each home was provided a lamb (Exod. 12:4). The second instruction was to count when Israel planted the new fruit trees after possessing the Promised Land, as the fruit was not to be eaten for three years. By the fourth year, the fruit was separated as holy to the Lord; and in the fifth year, the farmer was permitted to eat the fruit from his trees (Lev. 19:23-25). The third count was for counting the omer from Passover to Pentecost (Lev. 23:14-15). This fourth count is connected to the year of Jubilee, where a man who had given up his land inheritance could redeem it back on the year of Jubilee, or every fifty years. There was a counting of the years of the sale and the years remaining before the Jubilee cycle (Lev. 25:27; 52).

The day before the first reaping of the omer, officials went out to a special field near the Temple where selected men marked the first ripened grain, tying them into three bundles to make it easier to reap the following day. The reapers could not cut the grain until the sun was set—or as night was about to approach. Jewish sources indicate that on the first day of counting the omer, the villages surrounding Jerusalem gathered near the Temple for the ceremony. Three reapers were used, each with a separate sickle and basket. They asked the people gathered if the sun was setting and if the sickles and the baskets were ready. The collected barley grain was roasted with fire each day at the Temple.

Christ was crucified at Passover and arose during the time of the beginning of the counting of the omer, which was the beginning of the Feast of First Fruits of the barley presented to God. When Christ arose, there were also an unknown number of saints who arose with Him. These raised saints would be the first count of the omer, or the first fruits of the resurrection. They would be presented to God in His heavenly Temple when Christ ascended to heaven between the time He saw Mary, and the time the ten disciples saw Him later that day (compare John 20:17 and John 20:19). Christ Himself is called the first fruits of them that slept (1 Cor. 15:20).

GETTING THE LEAVEN OUT

The many often-concealed clues within the procedures of Israel's Feasts recorded in the Torah also should have a New Testament counterpart or fulfillment in a type or shadow. How does the daily count of the omer, and presenting the new ripened grain in the Temple, hold a prophetic imagery?

First the barley harvest is timed near Passover (redemption), followed the next day by Unleavened Bread. The words *leaven* or *leavened* are mentioned thirty-seven times in the Bible, and almost always represent sin or evil, including a doctrine which is corrupt. From Passover to the conclusion of First Fruits, all leaven was removed from the house of every Hebrew (for 7 days). Literal leaven was yeast that caused the dough to ferment and rise. The Unleavened bread used at Passover is flat bread baked without leaven, or before leaven has the time to raise the dough.

Christ was the bread from heaven and bread of life (John 6:22-59), and He was without sin (2 Cor. 5:21; Heb. 4:15). Even in the Torah Law, the blood of a sacrifice was not to be offered with leaven, with the exception of the peace and wave offerings (Exod. 23:18; 34:25; Lev. 7:13; 23:15-17). Paul wrote that a "little leaven leaveneth the whole lump" (Gal. 5:9), meaning that a little sin will spread fast, like leaven in dough. Paul used unleavened bread as a powerful analogy for victory over sin:

> *"Therefore purge out the old leaven, that you may be a new lump, since you truly are unleavened. For indeed Christ, our Passover, was sacrificed for us. Therefore let us keep the feast, not with old leaven, nor with the leaven of malice and wickedness, but with the unleavened bread of sincerity and truth."*

> – 1 COR. 5:7-8 (NKJV)

The barley is linked with Passover, and Passover is the feast of redemption where the blood of Christ our Lamb was shed to cleanse us from our sins. Thus, after Passover we receive freedom from past sins, as well as a cleansing *through repentance* for future sins (remember that Christ told the churches in Revelation to *repent*).

What is the prophetic connection with unleavened bread? The tribulation is one prophetic "week" or seven years in length (Dan. 9:27). Believers are to have their loins gird and lamps burning (Luke 12:35), and garments free from spots [sins], wrinkles [weights], and blemishes [moral corruption] (Eph. 5:27). We are to be bread without leaven, or believers who are free from the bondage of practicing a sinful life. Unleavened bread is required to be eaten for seven days. The true believers will be in heaven for seven years while the tribulation is raging during a seven-year timeframe on earth. All leaven is removed and taken from the house, freeing the family from the picture of evil and sin.

DECORATING THE BRIDE

The wonderful story of Ruth and Boaz transpired during both the barley and wheat harvests in Bethlehem (Ruth 2:23). Ruth arrived at the beginning of the barley harvest, and the marriage proposal happened at the beginning of the wheat harvest. This means that Ruth, who is a picture of the Gentile church (she was Gentile, not Jewish), and Boaz, a kinsman-redeemer who is a picture of Christ, were harvesting the barley during the seasons of counting the omer. Our omer season is to go into the entire world and preach the gospel to every person (Matt. 24:14), and bring in the harvest of souls from the field of the world, just as Ruth gleaned each day from the fields of Boaz. When the wheat harvest was collected, there was a wedding proposal and Ruth married her kinsman–redeemer. When Ruth stayed the night on the threshing floor with Boaz, this was during the wheat harvest (Ruth 3:1-14).

Among devout Jews, Ruth is read prior to the arrival of the Feast of Pentecost. There is also another Jewish custom of staying up all night to "decorate the bride." The reason many mystics stay up all night reading the law or various rabbinical commentaries is because, at midnight, Ruth was found at the feet of Boaz. Some Jews will conclude reading at midnight, and others will continue until the morning of Pentecost. The Zohar, a commentary of Jewish mysticism, calls the time between Passover and Pentecost, "the counting days of the bridegroom of Israel with the bride." In Jewish synagogues, the scroll of Ruth is read, since Ruth embraced the Jewish Law, and the harvest cycles are linked to the Feast of Weeks.

In the time of Christ, when a man was engaged to a woman, they did not date or visit each other during the entire time of their engagement. The father of the groom determined the day and hour when his son could return to his future bride's house and secretly take her in a procession to his house for the seven-day celebration and consummation of the marriage, which occurred at his father's house.

In Matthew 25, Christ spoke of ten virgins who were waiting for the bridegroom to arrive. These ten were actually bridesmaids who remained with the bride during the time she was waiting for her bridegroom, but were also responsible for her preparations of getting dressed to meet her bridegroom.

In ancient times, many marriages were conducted on Tuesday—the third day of the week. Rabbis noted that on the six days of creation, God blessed the third day with a double "it was good" (Gen. 1:10. 12). The double "good" pronounced on this day gave rise to the thought that a double blessing was assigned to the day; thus it was desirable to marry on this day. Pentecost often falls in the month of June, and thus the popular term—June bride.

THE WASHING OF THE BRIDE

Prior to the time that Ruth met Boaz on his threshing floor, where the grain was harvested and would later be separated and gathered into Boaz's storage jars, Ruth prepared herself for the meeting:

> *"Therefore wash yourself and anoint yourself, put on your best garment and go down to the threshing floor; but do not make yourself known to the man until he has finished eating and drinking."*
>
> – RUTH 3:3 (NKJV)

Every ancient Jewish bride required preparation before her wedding. This included a ceremonial washing in the mikveh, which was cut out of natural stone and held either rain or spring water. Throughout a Jewish woman's life, ritual washing was required each month after her menstrual cycle ended. This washing signified that the woman and her husband agreed to sexual relations, seven days after the conclusion of her cycle. Submerging in the mikveh was also required for any scribe working on a Torah Scroll, for anyone who was ceremonially unclean, and for all men entering the Temple at Jerusalem.

When Jesus attended the wedding in Canaan (John 2), the host ran out of wine. Jesus took six water pots made of stone and told servants to fill them with water, where He later turned the spring water into wine. In most Jewish villages clay vessels were common, which has been proven in excavations throughout Israel. In the wedding narrative, the six pots were "after the manner of the purification of the Jews" (John 2:6). These six stone pots would probably have been used by those attending the wedding to wash their hands before eating, or to purify other vessels and articles of furniture (Matt. 15:2; Luke 11:39; Mark 7:3-4). Another suggestion is that these same pots could have been used to bring spring water to pour into a mikveh, where the bride could wash before her wedding. The point is, there was a washing and cleansing ritual before people could enter the wedding.

Ruth was instructed to prepare for meeting Boaz by washing herself, anointing herself, and putting on her best garments (Ruth 3:3). These are the same instructions given to the bride of Christ—the church (2 Cor. 11:2). Paul said that we are sanctified and cleansed with the washing of the water of the Word (Eph. 5:26). The washing is to remove the spiritual spots, stains, and hidden sins so that our wedding garments will be clean and white, and we can stand before God in righteousness. The anointing is the Holy Spirit's presence given to us, which is the oil needed in the lamps of the ten virgins who are preparing to meet the bridegroom (see Matt. 25).

Christ will return for those who are looking for Him (Heb. 9:28); praying for His return (Mark 13:33); and praying to be worthy to escape the things which will come to pass on the earth (Luke 21:36).

The next feast to be fulfilled is the Feast of Trumpets. Without a doubt, this feast has strong allusions to the trumpets that will be blasted at the resurrection of the dead in Christ and the transformation of those who are alive at the return of Christ (1 Thessalonians 4:16-17).

CHAPTER 5

THE DAY OF ATONEMENT AND THE TRIBULATION CODE

I F THE GATHERING together of the saints (Eph. 1:9-10) were to occur on or near the season of the Feast of Trumpets, then the next major prophetic event that follows will be the beginning of the seven-year tribulation. This event will officially begin when, in heaven, Christ breaks the first seal of an ancient, seven-sealed heavenly scroll (see Rev. 5). These seven seals are parallel to the seven years of tribulation on earth.

Many scholars believe this seven-year timeframe is based upon Daniel 9:27 (one prophetic week of seven years), and upon the division of two timeframes in the Apocalypse's division of forty-two months and forty-two months, or 1,260 days and another 1,260 days (Rev. 11:2-6; 12:6; 13:5). Several interesting parallels link the ten-day period of time between Trumpets and the beginning of the next feast, the Day of Atonement. Known by its Hebrew name, Yom Kippur *(kaphar being translated as the Hebrew word for atonement),* this day was set aside each year for the High Priest, Levites, and Israelites to experience atonement, or the removal of their sins.

The Feast of Trumpets begins on the first day of the seventh month, and Atonement begins on the tenth day of the seventh month. This gives us a period of seven to eight days (in the ancient time) between the two feasts. In the days of the Jewish Temple, the High Priest participated in the blowing of the Trumpets. However, following this feast, the High Priest was required to separate himself from the Levites and the people in a special chamber in the Temple to prepare for the coming Day of Atonement. For the High Priest, the Levities (all of the other priests), and the common people (Israelites), this was a highly anticipated and fearful day. On this day, God would determine if He would *forgive the sins* of the people, or if He would *condemn them*. Moses wrote:

> *"Also on the tenth day of this seventh month there shall be a day of atonement: it shall be a holy convocation unto you; and ye shall afflict your souls, and offer an offering made by fire unto the LORD.*
>
> *And ye shall do no work in that same day: for it is a day of atonement, to make an atonement for you before the LORD your God."*
>
> – LEVITICUS 23:27-28

This was the only day of the Jewish year that the High Priest entered past the main veil into the Holy of Holies where, in Moses's tabernacle and Solomon's Temple, the golden Ark of the Covenant rested upon a rock. (The Ark was missing from the Temple in Christ's time, hidden perhaps before the Babylonian invasion.) Throughout the year, the High Priest wore his eight-piece garments of beauty, which included the golden breastplate with the twelve stones and the golden crown inscribed with "Holy unto the Lord" (see Exod. 28). On this one day however, the priest removed these royal garments and wore four specially woven linen garments: linen pants, a linen robe, a linen belt, and a linen bonnet (Lev. 16:4, 32). Jewish sages believed that the eight garments the High Priest wore throughout the year provided a complete picture of atonement for mankind. For example:

- The tunic, which covers the priest's body, atoned for killing.

- The pants atoned for sexual transgression.

- The turban, worn on the head, atoned for haughtiness.

- The belt atoned for sins of the heart.

- The breastplate atoned for errors in judgment.

- The ephod atoned for idolatry.

- The robe atoned for evil speech.

- The crown atoned for arrogance.

During the Day of Atonement process, the priest would offer a bull and two goats (see Lev. 16). He would enter the Holy of Holies three times with blood; once for himself, once for the Levites, and once for the Israelites.

Rabbis believe the prophet Daniel gave a perfect imagery of the Day of Atonement, which was occurring before the throne of God in heaven as individuals were preparing to be judged. Various terms found in these verses seem to match the details that occur on the Day of Atonement:

> *"I watched till thrones were put in place, and the Ancient of Days was seated; His garment was white as snow, and the hair of His head was like pure wool. His throne was a fiery flame, its wheels a burning fire; a fiery stream issued and came forth from before Him. A thousand thousands ministered to Him; ten thousand times ten thousand stood before Him. The court was seated, and the books were opened."*
>
> – Daniel 7:9-10 (NKJV)

The Day of Atonement is man's arrival in the heavenly court, when all people stand before God to receive a verdict. At the Jewish Temple, the High Priest stood for the entire Day of Atonement service, along with all the people. None were permitted to be seated until their guilt was cleared, they were forgiven, and atonement was finished. Note that today, Christ is seated at the right hand of God and is the High Priest of the new covenant (Heb. 1:3; Heb. 7:25). Christ sitting indicates that His priestly, atoning work has been accomplished.

According to rabbinical tradition, on the Day of Atonement, there were three types of individuals in Israel: the *totally righteous* whose names were inscribed in the heavenly book; the *totally unrighteous* whose names were not found in the book of life; and those who were *neither righteous nor unrighteous*, but must make a decision to choose between being righteous, or continuing in their sin and being unrighteous. The righteous names are inscribed in the book of life, while the other names are removed and the people marked for destruction— without repentance. On this special day, the totally righteous would be declared righteous and cleared of any wrong or guilt; the totally unrighteousness who did not repent would be condemned; and those living between the two would be required to either choose life (righteousness) or choose death (unrighteousness).

THE IMAGERY OF THE COMING TRIBULATION

When we explore the details and traditions linked with the Day of Atonement, the imagery clearly shows that this feast is a picture of the judgments prepared by God against the unrighteous on earth during the coming tribulation. Even the book of Revelation, John's apocalyptic vision that describes events during the tribulation (chapters 4–19), reveals there are three different types of people on earth at the time of the end. There are the totally righteous, who can be identified as the 144,000 Jews who are sealed with the seal of God that supernaturally protects them during the first forty-two months of the tribulation (Rev. 7).

Then we find the totally unrighteous, who are evil and wicked men who will not repent of their sins and evil deeds. These are destined to either die during the tribulation, or receive the mark of the beast and later be removed from the earth when Christ and His angels separate the wheat from the tares (Matt. 13:30).

The third group will be those with soiled garments who missed the initial return of Christ for the righteous on earth, and they make their robes white in the blood of Christ and are willing to die as martyrs for the gospel (Rev. 6:9; 7:14; 20:4).

It is important to note that the chief substance emphasized on the Day of Atonement is the blood of animals required to expiate the sins of the High Priest, Levites and Israelites. During the tribulation, the global judgment against the nations is partially for their shedding of human blood. For 2,000 years the descendants of those standing at

Pilate's judgment hall shed the blood of the prophets; shed the blood of the righteous saints; and shed the blood of Christ.

According to the words of Christ, Jerusalem was destroyed in AD 70 for shedding the blood of the prophets and righteous men sent to hear from God (Matt. 23:34-39). In the Old Testament, one of the final kings before the destruction of Jerusalem by Nebuchadnezzar was Manasseh, who "filled Jerusalem with innocent blood" (2 Kings 24:4). The chronicles of the kings of Israel and Judah make it clear that one of the reasons Jerusalem was destroyed was the shedding of the blood of innocent poor and righteous people, and God would not pardon this terrible scourge on the land (2 Kings 24).

In the Apocalypse, we read that during the coming tribulation, the world is judged for slaying the righteous. In chapter 6 there are martyrs under the golden altar in heaven who are asking the Almighty how long it will be until they are avenged of their shed blood (Rev. 6:10-11). Even the religious city labeled Mystery Babylon is destroyed because she was found guilty of the blood of Christ, the saints, and the prophets (Rev. 18:24).

On the Day of Atonement, the High Priest would stand at the Eastern Gate, which was the main gate to the Temple from the Mount of Olives, and watch the procession of animals that would be sacrificed on the brass altar. Elders were assigned to watch the High Priest as he observed the animals. Throughout the book of Revelation, at the Temple of God in heaven, there are elders sitting on twenty-four thrones observing the activities, from the breaking of the seals on the large seven-sealed scroll (Rev. 5), to the seven vial and trumpets judgments, and to the very destruction of Mystery Babylon.

Part of the Day of Atonement was certainly fulfilled through Christ, as His blood cleansed, forgave, and redeemed us from our sins. However, there is another aspect of the Day of Atonement, and that is judgment on the unrighteous that must occur on this day.

According to Jewish reckoning, the Temple of Solomon stood for 410 years, with a total of twelve High Priests ministering in this Temple. However, after the Jews returned from Babylon, the Temple stood for 420 years, from the rebuilding by Ezra and Nehemiah until the destruction in AD 70. There were three hundred High Priests during this 420-year period. The reason only twelve ministered at the first Temple and over three hundred at the second Temple is because the glory and fear of God was upon those from Solomon to the destruction, and God gave them long life to minister. In the second Temple, there was a strong spiritual decline, with corruption and sin among the priests. Thus they were spiritually unfit to offer the atoning blood, and their lives were taken earlier than their predecessors.

THE WHITE GARMENTS

On the Day of Atonement, the High Priest was robed in four white linen garments the entire day that he ministered at the Temple in Jerusalem. Christ is our High Priest in heaven, and in Revelation chapter one, John saw Christ with a garment draping His body down to His feet. The word *garment* in the New Testament is the word *himation*, which is considered to be an outer dress (like a cloak) or some form of a robe (Matt. 14:36; 22:11). Christ's *garment* is the word *poderes*, which is of uncertain affinity and means a garment that reached to the ankles.

In heaven, martyrs will wear white robes (Rev. 6:11), and those coming out of great tribulation will also be clothed with white robes (Rev. 7:9). When the seven angels exit the heavenly Temple with the last seven bowls of wrath, these angels are clothed in white linen with golden belts around their chest (Rev. 15:6). The white linen worn by believers represents the righteousness of the saints (Rev. 19:8). When worn by these angels, white linen indicates that the judgments being poured out are the image of a Day of Atonement, when the High Priest wears linen to perform his duties.

THE GOLDEN ALTAR

Another clue in the Apocalypse that marks the Day of Atonement imagery is the activity at the heavenly golden altar. On the regular days at the Temple, a priest was selected to offer the morning incense on the golden altar through a process called *casting lots*. On the Day of Atonement, however, the High Priest himself offered the incense as part of the ritual. In Revelation chapter 8, we read of the heavenly golden altar and incense:

> *"When He opened the seventh seal, there was silence in heaven for about half an hour. And I saw the seven angels who stand before God, and to them were given seven trumpets. Then another angel, having a golden censer, came and stood at the altar. He was given much incense, that he should offer it with the prayers of all the saints upon the golden altar which was before the throne. And the smoke of the incense, with the prayers of the saints, ascended before God from the angel's hand. Then the angel took the censer, filled it with fire from the altar, and threw it to the earth. And there were noises, thunderings, lightnings, and an earthquake."*
>
> – REV. 8:1-5 (NKJV)

Many scholars believe this angel was Christ at the golden altar, as He alone is the High Priest of heaven making intercession for us (Heb. 7:25). On the Day of Atonement, the unrighteous will be judged for not repenting and turning to God. According to rabbis, the prayers of Jews and believing Gentiles who had received the God of Abraham as their God would travel to the golden altar. Each morning all the words of the people would ascend into heaven through the "holy smoke" that came from the burning incense on the altar. Notice that the angel in Revelation 8 uses a *golden censer* for the incense, the same golden type which was used by the High Priest on the Day of Atonement.

When the angel took the incense in the golden censer and cast it to the earth, it was a sign that the prayers of the saints for vengeance against the ungodly and those shedding innocent blood would be vindicated upon those who martyred the righteous on earth (Rev. 6:9-11). The judgment is released to earth the moment that the holy fire strikes the holy incense, and the messenger of the Lord throws the censer to the earth.

The additional evidence that this event is linked with the Day of Atonement is the phrase, thirty minutes of silence in heaven (Rev. 8:1). When Aaron made atonement on the Day of Atonement, there was silence among the people and not rejoicing, as they were uncertain of God's response to them.

On the Day of Atonement, two goats were presented to the High Priest: one was marked for the Lord and the other, identified as the scapegoat, was marked for Azzazel. At some point during the priestly ritual, the High Priest placed his hands upon the scapegoat, symbolically transferring the sins of Israel upon the goat's head. This goat would then be led by the priest to a cliff in the wilderness, known as the Mount of the Azzazel, where the goat would be hurled off the high mountain and killed. This was done so that the sin goat would never find its way back to an Israeli village or city, and thereby carry back the forgiven sins of the people. Once the sins are forgiven, they are not to be brought up or remembered again (Isa. 43:25); thus, the goat had to be thrown from the sacred mountain to the earth below.

This parallel is also discovered in Revelation chapter 12, during a cosmic battle between the archangel Michael and his angels, and Satan and his angels. Michael will literally hurl (that is, cast out—verse 9) Satan from the second heaven to the earth at some point during the seven-year tribulation (Rev. 12:7-19). One reason for the removal of Satan from the cosmic realm is to prevent him from continuing as an "accuser of the brethren before God" (Rev. 12:10). Just as the sins of the scapegoat are not permitted to be seen again after the death of the goat, so at this point in the tribulation—with the prophets, saints and those who fear the Lord in heaven (Rev. 11:18)—Satan is no longer permitted on the Mountain of God in heaven, but is cast down to earth where God has restricted his presence.

There was only one time a year when the High Priest was permitted to see the golden Ark of the Covenant behind the veil in the sacred chamber called the Holy of Holies, and that was on the Day of Atonement. On this day, the High Priest sprinkled the sacrificial blood on the east side of the mercy seat, which was the golden lid covering the contents inside the Ark. There is only one mention of the heavenly Ark of the Covenant in the book of Revelation. We read:

> *"And the temple of God was opened in heaven, and there was seen in his temple the ark of his testament: and there was lightning, and voices, and thunder, and an earthquake, and great hail."*
>
> – Revelation 11:19 (NKJV)

The Ark in heaven is made visible only after the doors of the Temple are opened, as preparations are made for the final seven angels to enter the Temple and release the vial (or bowl) judgments (Rev. 16). In this setting, the doors of the Temple swing open and the Ark is viewed by the heavenly dwellers, as the judgment of the saints in heaven is about to begin. We read:

> *"And the nations were angry, and thy wrath is come, and the time of the dead, that they should be judged, and that you should give reward unto your servants the prophets, and to the saints, and them that fear thy name, small and great; and should destroy them which destroy the earth."*
>
> – Revelation 11:18 (KNJV)

Since the Ark was only visible to the High Priest during the yearly atonement process—a time when God judged His people—then the visibility of the Ark in this passage identifies another imagery of the Day of Atonement. The saints are being judged, the nations of the earth are angry, and the wrath of God is being poured out upon the earth.

The book of Revelation reveals that earthly judgments are released from the heavenly Temple through the seven sealed book (Rev. 5), the seven trumpet judgments (Rev. 7-10), and the seven vial judgments (Rev. 16). These judgments are being initiated as the heavenly judge has pronounced guilt upon the nations for slaying the righteous and for sinning against God's Word. Thus, the judgments of the tribulation fit the patterns of the sixth feast of Israel, the Day of Atonement.

THE NUMBERS AND LINKS TO THE FEASTS

While the following information is not a theological revelation or a doctrine to be built upon, it is an interesting observation based upon the order of the feasts. I have stated that numbers have significant meaning in the Bible, as God is the originator of minutes, hours, days, years, time, colors, numbers and all things. The Feast of Pentecost is the *fourth* feast of Israel, and the number four is a cardinal and earthly number—one river parting into four rivers in Eden (Gen. 2:10); four directions of earth: north, south, east and west; and four gospels cover the earthly ministry of Christ.

The fifth feast is Trumpets, and five is the Biblical number referring to the grace of God. David picked up five smooth stones from the brook before he faced Goliath (1 Sam. 17:40), and there is a fivefold office of ministry: apostle, prophet, pastor, evangelist, and teacher assigned for the edification and growth of the church (Eph. 4:11-12). We are presently living in the church age, or the dispensation of the grace of God (see Eph. 3:2). The church age will conclude with the return of Christ at the gathering together. This is also when the dispensation of grace concludes and the season of judgment is released on earth. Thus, during the fifth feast, the church will experience the grace of God by removing us from the wrath to come (Luke 21:36; 1 Thess. 5:9).

As indicated earlier, mankind's number is identified with six, as Adam was created on the sixth day. In the Apocalypse, the future beast (the antichrist and his system) is linked with the number six hundred, sixty and six (Rev. 13:18). The sixth feast of Israel, the Day of Atonement, centered on the entire nation of Israel. The tribulation's link to the sixth feast is significant, when considering there are six judgment seals, six trumpets that initiate judgments, and six vials that angels pour out upon the earth.

As the seventh seal is broken by Christ, there is silence in heaven and a transition to the trumpet judgments (Rev. 8:1-2). The seventh trumpet blast announces that the mystery of God is finished (Rev. 10:7), and the angel with the seventh vial (bowl) announces, "It is done" (Rev. Rev. 16:17). Thus, each six is the climax of a particular series of judgments being released.

Seven is the Biblical number of completion and even perfection in the kingdom. The seventh feast of Israel is Tabernacles, the feast in which the kingdoms of this world will become the kingdoms of God, and He will rule on earth for a thousand years. Just as God rested on the seventh day, mankind and all resurrected Believers will enter into a season of rest, and men will cease from war.

These numerical links with the fall feasts can also be observed with the spring feasts. The Bible indicates that Christ was crucified near the time of Passover, was three days and nights in the heart of the earth, and was raised again on the third day (Acts 10:40). This places the timing of Christ being seen alive by His disciples, Peter and John, at the day after the Sabbath, which would be a Sunday morning. At that time on the Jewish calendar, this would have been the first day of the week, since the Saturday Sabbath was the seventh day.

The third feast was First Fruits, which began the day after the Sabbath—again, Sunday morning—when the High Priest at the Temple presented the first ripened barley grain before the Lord and offered a lamb on the brass altar. Christ arose on the third day at the beginning of the third feast. He was the first fruits of those who slept, as it is written, *"But now is Christ risen from the dead, and become the first fruits of them that slept"* (1 Cor. 15:20).

Oddly, the numerical order of the feasts—Passover (the first) and Tabernacles (the seventh) have certain links to the feast number, the chronological order, and the numbers connected with the events on the particular feast. Again, this is not meant to forge a doctrine, but only as a point of interest.

THE SEVEN-DAY PREPARATION

In this teaching, I identify the Feast of Trumpets with blasts of the shofar to raise the dead in Christ and to change the bodies of those living from mortality to immortality. Then there are nine days from the conclusion of Trumpets to the beginning of the Day of Atonement. The theme of the Day of Atonement is judgment or forgiveness; God will either begin to judge Israel, or He will forgive their sins and iniquities. Atonement rituals reveal the coming great tribulation on earth where the wrath of the Lamb (Rev. 6:16), wrath of God (Rev. 14:10), and wrath of Satan (Rev. 12:12) merge on earth during a seven-year season.

Between the days concluding the Feast of Trumpets to the beginning of Atonement, there was a priestly custom established that mirrors the Believers being separated in heaven from those on earth. Seven days before Yom Kippur, the High Priest would leave his home and separate himself from all others in a special room at the Temple, *Lishkas Ha'ets*, or *Lishkas Parhedrin*, (High Priest's chamber) located along the northern wall. This separation was required to prepare him for approaching God in the Holy of Holies, and rehearsing in his mind the details required of him to enact the rituals for the Atonement.

On the third and seventh day, he was sprinkled with the ashes of the *parah-adummoh* (red heifer) mixed with water for a water of purification (see Numbers 19). He sat with two other priests who were knowledgeable in all procedures, and reviewed in detail each step— the offering, sprinkling of blood, and prayer—as this was Israel's most important day before God.

The prophet Isaiah gave an astonishing prediction of the coming resurrection and future tribulation when the judgments of the Lord are released upon the earth:

> *"Your dead shall live; together with my dead body they shall arise. Awake and sing, you who dwell in dust; for your dew is like the dew of herbs, and the earth shall cast out the dead.*
>
> *"Come, my people, enter your chambers, and shut your doors behind you; Hide yourself, as it were, for a little moment, until the indignation is past. For behold, the LORD comes out of His place to punish the inhabitants of the earth for their iniquity; the earth will also disclose her blood, and will no more cover her slain."*
>
> – ISA. 26:19-21 (NKJV)

Isaiah foresaw the resurrection of the righteous, which in the New Testament occurs when Christ gathers together the church—those on earth and in heaven (1 Thess. 4:16-17). The earth "casting out the dead" is similar to the phrases, "the sea gave up the dead...and death and hell delivered up the dead..." (Rev. 20:13). Isaiah then commands God's people to shut your doors and hide yourself until the indignation (wrath) is over.

Isaiah predicted that God was coming out of His place to punish those dwelling on the earth. This instruction can have a dual application. First, a remnant of Jews during the tribulation will flee into hiding in the wilderness and be protected until the tribulation passes and Christ returns (see Rev. 12). Second, the saints will be separated from those on earth and taken to heaven where they will be protected during the indignation and release of God's wrath upon the earth.

Part of the reason for the future judgment is to judge the earth for the shedding of innocent blood. When Cain killed Abel, his blood cried out to God for revenge (Gen. 4:10). Christ pronounced a curse upon Jerusalem for shedding the blood of the prophets and righteous men, and predicted the city would be destroyed in a generation because of this sin (Matt. 23:34-37). In the future, a false religious system called mystery Babylon the great is destroyed in one hour, as she is guilty of shedding the blood of saints and prophets (Rev. 16:6).

How can Believers "enter into their chambers?" The Hebrew word refers to an inner chamber room or some form of a dwelling place like an apartment. The priest, in preparation for the time of judgment (atonement), hides himself in a chamber at the Temple. For those who believe in a pre-tribulation ingathering, believers—who are called kings and priest unto God (Rev. 5:10)—will be gathered at the Father's house in heaven during the seven years, just as the High Priest was hidden in a private chamber for seven days.

The High Priest would exit the chamber on the Day of Atonement and perform his duties according to the Law and custom. The saints will come out of their heavenly dwelling at the end of the seven years, as the final judgment is given to the earth and the Messiah returns with the saints to deliver the remnant of Jews from their destruction, and to judge the antichrist, false prophet, and beast system—all in one day!

Consider the Jewish wedding. During the wedding ceremony the couple stands under a large cloth that is held up by four poles and carried by four men. This cloth is called a *chuppah*, meaning, canopy or covering. The chuppah represents the home the couple will build together. It is open on all four sides, reminding the couple of Abraham's tent, which was open to all for hospitality. The chuppah has no furniture, to remind the newlyweds that it is not the furniture that makes up the house, but it is the people in the house. Most importantly, the chuppah represents the Divine covering and protection of God over the house and the couple, and the presence of God over the covenant of marriage.

In early times, the Jewish wedding was consummated in a private room which was called a chuppah. The ancient wedding was celebrated for an entire week. Just as the bride and groom celebrated their future together for one week, during the final prophetic week the church, as the bride of Christ, will celebrate in the Father's house during the entire week.

Some have pointed out that the priest is concealed for seven days and not seven years, and the Jewish wedding continues for seven days and not seven years. But in the Bible, we see a pattern of days becoming years. In the Old Testament, twelve men spied the land for forty days, and ten of them returned to the camp with a negative report. This caused the Israelites to return to the wilderness and wander in circles for forty years, until all the generation of unbelievers died in the desert (except Joshua and Caleb). For every day in unbelief (forty) God gave them a year of punishment:

> *"According to the number of the days in which you spied out the land, forty days, for each day you shall bear your guilt one year, namely forty years, and you shall know My rejection."*
>
> – NUM. 14:34-35 (NKJV)

God took each day and turned it into a year of straying in the desert. A second example of a year representing a day is found in Ezekiel 4:4-6 (NJKV):

> *"Lie also on your left side, and lay the iniquity of the house of Israel upon it. According to the number of the days that you lie on it, you shall bear their iniquity. For I have laid on you the years of their iniquity, according to the number of the days, three hundred and ninety days; so you shall bear the iniquity of the house of Israel. And when you have completed them, lie again on your right side; then you shall bear the iniquity of the house of Judah forty days. I have laid on you a day for each year."*

Thus, there is a Biblical precedent of each day becoming one year. In the case of Israel in the wilderness, their sin was unbelief; and in the time of Ezekiel, the sin was iniquity. The tribulation will be the climax of man's iniquity on earth, or the cup of iniquity being full (Dan. 8:23), and men will no longer repent (Rev. 16:11). Instead of judging the earth for seven days, seven years are required to purge the earth (Isa 13).

If the gathering together of the church occurs on the Feast of Trumpets, then the next feast in chronological order is the Day of Atonement. The time of tribulation will follow the great catching away; thus, the order of the feasts indicates the order of future events. The rapture on the Feast of Trumpets is followed by the tribulation, as we will find concealed in the patterns of the Day of Atonement.

CHAPTER 6

THE FUTURE GREAT ASSEMBLY

THIS SECTION WILL detail a lesser known command given to the Israelites to gather at the Temple every seven years for the Great Assembly. This Great Assembly is a beautiful picture of the gathering together of the saints of God—both Gentiles and Jews—in heaven. In the days of the Temple, every seven years was a sabbatical for the entire land of Israel. We read:

> *"Six years you shall sow your land and gather in its produce, but the seventh year you shall let it rest and lie fallow, that the poor of your people may eat; and what they leave, the beasts of the field may eat."*
>
> – Exod. 23:10-11 (NKJV)

> *"But in the seventh year there shall be a sabbath of solemn rest for the land, a sabbath to the LORD. You shall neither sow your field nor prune your vineyard. What grows of its own accord of your harvest you shall not reap, nor gather the grapes of your untended vine, for it is a year of rest for the land."*
>
> – Lev. 25:4-6 (NKJV)

Every seventh year was designated as a year of rest for all the land. Also, every seventh year the Great Assembly occurred. The primary purpose was to strengthen the entire community of Israel spiritually by encouraging them to study the Law and observe God's commandments. Nearly all men, women and children were involved, and the *gerim*—a Hebrew word for *male foreigner*—who converted to Judaism were also invited. This is a noticeable difference, as the three main feasts were attended by all males over age twenty. Women could attend, but it was voluntary and not obligatory. The family of Jesus, including His mother Mary and their friends—attended these feasts (Luke 2:41).

But at the Great Assembly the entire family was present. When the saints gather together in heaven, John identified them as "out of every nation, kindred, tongue and people" (Rev. 7:9).

Called the Hakhel (Great Assembly), the event took place following the seventh year (Jubilee), on the beginning of the eighth year. During the Great Assembly, the huge multitude gathered together at the sound of gold trumpet blasts.

This is the second noticeable indicator, as all other feasts and holy days were introduced by the sounds of the shofar (horn of an animal) or the silver trumpets (see Num. 10:2-10). Here, gold trumpets were sounded. Gold is the most valuable of precious metals, and the Ark of the Covenant, the menorah, the golden altar, and table of showbread were made of gold, or wood covered with gold. Gold never fades or tarnishes and was fought over by empires throughout history because of its value. Gold represents God and His Divine nature.

When the church is caught up to meet the Lord in the air at the gathering together (1 Thess. 4:16-17; Eph. 1:9-10), the Lord Himself descends with the "trump of God" (1 Thess. 4:16). The only allusion to God and a trumpet in the Bible is in Exodus 19:19-20. The voice of God sounds similar to the blast of a trumpet, such as on Mount Sinai where the moment the voice of the trumpet grew louder and longer, God came down and Moses went up. When the trump of God blasts its sound, the Lord will descend and we will be caught up to meet Him in the air (1 Thess. 4:17). Since a gold trumpet was used to gather the Great Assembly at the Temple Mount, then it is possible the trump of God is a gold trumpet; not a silver one, nor the horn of an animal.

On this day in Jerusalem a large platform, called a *bimah* (which is *bema* in Greek), was erected in the center of the Temple Mount, just below the fifteen steps outside the doors of the main house where the

Levitical choirs would assemble to sing. Once the crowds arrived, the king would ascend to the bema and be seated, as the sacred Torah scroll was carried by the head of the Temple Mount synagogue. He would give the scroll to the High Priest's deputy, who then passed the sacred books to the High Priest.

The High Priest would hand the Torah to the king, who stood up to receive the Torah, and then would remain standing to read aloud selected passages from the Word of God. The king would begin reading in Deuteronomy, the book with the moral, ceremonial and sacrificial laws of God, and read to the section that says you shall love the Lord and obey His voice (Deut. 30:20). The king could read the later portions while seated, but it was preferred that he stand.

The fact that the High Priest and the king were together on the same platform is significant, considering that Christ is presently the High Priest of our faith, ever living in heaven to make intercession for us (Heb. 7:25). Then in Revelation 19, He takes the new position of King of kings and Lord of lords (Rev. 19:16). Christ is a King after the order of Melchizedek, the first king-priest in the Bible, who was priest of God and king of Jerusalem (see Genesis 14). We know there is a judgment in Heaven called the judgment seat, or bema, of Christ (2 Cor. 5:10). This bema judgment occurs in heaven and is mentioned in Revelation 11:18.

How does the imagery of the Great Assembly with the king and the Torah scroll compare to the great gathering together in heaven? In John's apocalyptic vision, he saw the Lamb (Christ) take from the right hand of God a seven-sealed scroll that can only be opened and read by Christ Himself. As Christ breaks six seals, there is an announcement of six different judgments that will strike the earth—one judgment for each of the six seals. The breaking of the seventh seal transitions into three woes (see Revelation chapter 6-9). Christ the Priest breaks the seals, and this is the beginning of Christ's transition from a Priest to a King!

I believe Paul had the imagery of this Great Assembly in mind, when he wrote these words:

> *"But you have come to Mount Zion and to the city of the living God, the heavenly Jerusalem, to an innumerable company of angels, to the general assembly and church of the firstborn who are registered in heaven, to God the Judge of all, to the spirits of just men made perfect, to Jesus the Mediator of the new covenant, and to the blood of sprinkling that speaks better things than that of Abel."*
>
> – Hebrews 12:22-24 (NKJV)

Paul is speaking of the gathering of the saints, accompanied by angels, in the heavenly Mount Zion. The phrase, "the spirits of just men made perfect," refers to both the dead who were raised and the living who were changed from mortal to immortality.

Paul also uses a term for this meeting: the general assembly. In Greek this phrase is *paneguris*, which refers to a mass meeting, and also universal companionship. It can also refer to a festive gathering of people to celebrate public games or solemnities. It was used among the Greeks to describe the crowds gathered for the Olympic Games. Just as these Greek games were viewed by massive numbers of observers, in Paul's writings the spectators are the angels of God. Should the Rapture of the church occur during one of the feasts of Israel, then this assembly in heaven would literally be a festive gathering on a sacred festival appointed by God.

W.E. Vines points out that the Greek word *paneguris* comes from pan, meaning *all*, and agora, meaning *any kind of assembly*. He points out that the word refers to an assembly of all people, in contrast to the council of national elders, or the people gathering in honor of a god or a public festival such as the Olympic Games. The word church in Greek is *ekklesia*, meaning a *calling out*, which referred to a body of citizens who gathered to discuss the affairs of the state. In Israel, however, when the people were gathered together (such as at Mount Sinai), it was a national gathering and not a gathering of individual groups of people, such as would be in a local church.

Another word linked to assembling together is found in 2 Thessalonians 2:1 where Paul wrote: "Now, brethren, concerning the coming of our Lord Jesus Christ and our gathering together to Him…" The phrase *gathering together* is a direct reference to the church of called out believers, whose names are in the Lamb's book of life, being gathered together at the return of Christ. In 1 Thessalonians, we are *caught up together* (4:17), and in Ephesians we are *gathered together* in Christ, both those in heaven and in earth (Eph. 1:9-10).

In 2 Thessalonians 2:1 the phrase *gathering together* in Greek is *episunagoge*. The word is also used in Hebrews 10:25 when speaking of Believers on earth not forsaking the *assembling of yourselves together*. Christ used the word *episunago* when He said that He wanted to gather His people under His protection, as a hen gathers its chicks (Matt. 23:37). He also used the word in Matthew 24:31 when He spoke of gathering His elect from the four winds of heaven.

Paul spoke of the gathering together (episunagogue) unto Christ, which is the initial event of the dead in Christ being raised and the living being changed from mortality to immortality (1 Cor. 15:51-55), rising from earth to meet Christ in the air. Their arrival at the Temple of God in heaven, accompanied by the angels, is called the Great Assembly *(paneguris)*.

The scenes John gives us in Revelation are a clear parallel to the seven-year gatherings of Israel at Jerusalem's Temple. It is significant that Gentile converts were permitted on the mountain of God during this special gathering, just as the Jews and Gentiles alike will be welcomed at the Great Assembly when Christ brings us together to worship our Messiah, Priest and King in heaven.

CHAPTER 7

INSIGHT CONCEALED IN THE FEAST OF TABERNACLES

"Speak unto the children of Israel, saying, The fifteenth day of this seventh month shall be the Feast of Tabernacles for seven days unto the LORD.

On the first day shall be an holy convocation: ye shall do no servile work therein. Seven days ye shall offer an offering made by fire unto the LORD: on the eighth day shall be an holy convocation unto you; and ye shall offer an offering made by fire unto the LORD: it is a solemn assembly; and ye shall do no servile work therein."

- LEVITICUS 23:34-36

ISRAEL'S SEVENTH FEAST in Hebrew is called *Sukkot*, or in English, *Tabernacles*. This feast begins on the fifteenth day of the seventh month and continues for seven days, in which each day is accompanied by burnt offerings on the brass altar of sacrifice. Each feast has a specific designation commemorating a major event, and Tabernacles—also called Feast of Booths—commemorates the time that Israel dwelt outdoors in tents during their forty years in the wilderness. This feast also falls during the conclusion of the harvest cycle and the beginning of the rain and new winter planting season. During this feast, seventy bullocks are offered that represent the seventy souls that came out of Jacob (Exod. 1:5).

On the last day of Tabernacles, the priest who was on duty performed the water libation ceremony. The High Priest, dressed in his eight garments of beauty, descended from the Temple platform to the pool of Shiloah on the southern part of the slopes outside the city walls, and led a group of joyful priests through the water gate to the pool below. This pool contained living waters, meaning it was spring fed from flowing waters and not a stagnant pond of water. The High Priest would fill a golden vessel with the living water from the pool, and then return to the Temple through the Eastern Gate. Fellow priests had previously cut willow branches twenty-five feet in length. As the priest made his way back to the altar, each priest stood shoulder to shoulder, thirty feet apart, and moved their feet in unison as they swished the branches from left to right in unison.

This swishing action produced the sound of a "rushing wind," and was an illustration of the Holy Spirit's breath that would blow in the Temple. When the Holy Spirit blanketed Jerusalem on the Day of Pentecost, the believers were gathered in the Temple area when the Spirit descended like a mighty rushing wind (Acts 2:1-4). This wind was heard by those in the room, and it also would have gained the attention of the multitude gathered in the large court area.

During this unique ritual, a flute player—also termed *the pierced one*—called for both the wind and water to enter the Temple. Near the brass altar were two containers—one silver that held wine, and one gold that held the living water. At a precise moment in the ceremony, the High Priest mixed the wine and water into one vessel. Other priests circled the altar seven times, forming a willow canopy above the brass altar.

These yearly traditions held a specific implication for the Messiah. Christ would be pierced in His hands, feet and side, with blood dripping from the piercing of the thorns on His head. The prophet Zechariah predicted that the Jews would one day look upon Him whom they had pierced (Zech. 12:10). Christ is certainly the "pierced one" of Zechariah's prophecy.

The wine and water is significant, as wine in the Eucharist is symbolic of the blood of Christ (John 6:54-55; 1 Cor. 11:25). The community of priests at the Temple required daily ceremonial cleansing by the water of the laver, and each day they laid blood sacrifices on the altar. This imagery of blood and water is witnessed at the moment of Christ's death, as the Centurion thrust a spear into Christ's heart, sending forth blood and water (John 19:34). The mixing and eventual pouring out of the water and wine on the altar on the last day of the feast was a picture of Christ, who would bring forth the water and blood from His body, providing redemption at the altar of repentance. Through His blood we are saved and our sins are symbolically washed away through the water of baptism, as it is written:

> *"And now why are you waiting? Arise and be baptized, and wash away your sins, calling on the name of the Lord."*
>
> – ACTS 22:16 (NKJV)

THE LULAV

The rejoicing on Tabernacles is accompanied with an object called the lulav, which is made from the branches of four different trees mentioned in Leviticus 23:40. Each tree represents four experiences in life. The first branch is the palm branch, which is a Jewish picture of joy. Palms were used when Christ entered Jerusalem riding on a donkey, and palm branches are waved in heaven as those coming out of the tribulation rejoice in their victory over the beast kingdom (John 12:13; Rev. 7:9). A myrtle branch is tied with the palm branch, representing rest, as God gives rest to the people on the Sabbath cycles.

The willow branch has been a symbol of sorrow and weeping, as confirmed when the Jewish captives in Babylon hung their harps upon willow trees and refused to sing the Lord's song in a strange land (Ps. 137:1-9). The fourth branch is the citron, which is a citrus tree that is slightly bitter and sour, and represents times of bitterness.

Among the Ashkenazi Jews, three branches are used and a fruit, called an etrog (fruit from a citron tree) is added. This special branch is waved during the feast. In Christ's time, the waving was performed for the entire seven days of the feast.

JESUS ATTENDED THIS FEAST

According to John's gospel, Christ participated in the festivals during His lifetime. John records an important narrative occurring on the last day of the Feast of Tabernacles. This day was known as the "Day of the Great Hosanna." At this time, all of the leaves were shaken off the willow branches and the palms were beaten into pieces on the side of the altar. At the same time, the priest returned from the pool of Shiloah for the last time as the Hallel Psalms were sung and three blasts of the silver trumpets were heard. In Christ's day, as the people were worshipping the following occurred:

> *"In the last day, that great day of the feast, Jesus stood and cried, saying, If any man thirst, let him come unto me, and drink.*
>
> *He that believeth on me, as the scripture hath said, out of his belly shall flow rivers of living water. But this spake he of the Spirit, which they that believe on him should receive: for the Holy Ghost was not yet given; because that Jesus was not yet glorified."*
>
> – JOHN 7:37-39

The ceremony of the water libation occurs on the last day of the feast. In John's narrative, Christ is at the Temple near the brass altar as the High Priest is pouring out the wine and oil from the golden vessel and praying for the rains to come and the Spirit to be poured out. Suddenly there is a loud voice (Jesus cried out – verse 37), saying to come to Him and drink, for out of your belly will flow rivers of living water.

Somewhere, in this same location, would be where the Holy Spirit would blow like a wind and the Spirit would baptize the first believers in His power (Acts 1:8; 2:1-4). The Feast of Tabernacles and the libation service are designed to ask God for natural rain for the coming harvests and for spiritual rain in the form of the outpouring of the Holy Spirit. Water is poured upon the four corners of the altar, just as the Holy Spirit would be poured out globally on all four directions of the earth—north, south, east and west. Thus, Jesus connects the last day of tabernacles with the coming outpouring of the Spirit.

Even the Jewish Talmud states, "Why is the name of it called, the drawing out of water? Because of the pouring out of the Holy Spirit, according to what is said: 'With joy shall ye draw water from the wells of salvation.' " According to the same rabbinical authorities, the Holy Spirit dwells in many only through joy.

Notice that after the wine and water are mixed and the leaves from the branches are beaten, there is a cry from Christ that the Spirit is coming! The coming of the Spirit was preceded by the physical beating of the Messiah and the pouring of water and blood from His flesh. Christ's sufferings and resurrection provided the opportunity for God to send the other Comforter, the Holy Spirit to us (John 14:16; 16:7).

THE 8TH DAY OF THE FEAST

The Torah says this feast is to continue for seven days; however, an additional eighth day was added later. It is called Shemini Atzeret, (the eight day of Assembly) and includes Simchat Torah—the rejoicing in the Torah. Devout Jews read the Torah through in a yearly cycle. Simchat Torah celebrates the final reading of Deuteronomy 34, the last part of the Torah, and the return to the beginning of Torah in Genesis 1. It is a circle which beings in Genesis and ends in Deuteronomy, only to be repeated the following year. Jesus remained in Jerusalem at this time, and it was during this time that the religious leaders brought a woman to Him who was caught in the act of adultery (John 8:4).

Jesus had remained in Jerusalem for the night during the conclusion of the eighth day, spending the night on the Mount of Olives (John 8:1). In the morning He returned to the Temple for the eighth day, which would have been the rejoicing in the Torah. That morning the Pharisees threw at His feet a woman who had been caught in the act of adultery. The Law required that she be stoned, and the Pharisees demanded from Christ a response about the woman's deserved punishment. Instead of initiating a verbal argument, Christ gave an illustrated message by writing on the ground.

This is significant considering the trial of bitter waters, a ritual recorded in Numbers 5. If a husband suspected that his wife had secretly committed adultery and he could not prove it, he brought her to the priest who performed a rather bizarre ritual. The priest wrote the curses of the law on parchment. Then he mixed water with dirt from the floor, and poured the water over the curses, causing the words from the ink to enter a cup. The woman was required to drink this mixture. If she was not guilty, she would have no ill effect. If she was guilty, her thigh would begin to swell (Num. 5:12-31).

Since the trial of bitter waters would have been performed at the Temple, it could be that Christ actually wrote in the very dirt that would have been used during the trial for a woman accused by her husband of adultery. However, it is more likely that Christ's actions were found in this verse:

> *"O LORD, the hope of Israel, all who forsake You shall be ashamed. Those who depart from me shall be written in the earth because they have forsaken the LORD, the fountain of living water."*
>
> – JEREMIAH 17:13 (NKJV)

What would Christ have written that would have caused these accusers to lay down their stones and walk away in silence? Some speculate that Christ wrote the names of these religious accusers and began listing their sins, much to their embarrassment. One by one the stones were dropped and the violent mob dispersed, until only Christ and the woman remained. This incident, on the day of the rejoicing in the Torah, revealed that the living Torah, or living Word, was Christ Himself. Sinners could now rejoice in the Torah, as the Word made flesh was now manifest to deliver the sinner from sin and guilt. What religion failed to do—love the unlovable—Christ did.

TABERNACLES IN THE MILLENNIUM

The fall feasts carry the codes for future events. The Feast of Tabernacles is, unquestionably, a picture of the future kingdom of Christ on earth. The future rule of Christ with the saints on earth from Jerusalem is called the millennial reign, as it lasts for a thousand years (Rev. 20:2-6). According to the prophet Ezekiel, in the Messiah's kingdom, all believers and those in the world will keep the Sabbath, the new moons, and the special feasts during this time (Ezek. 45:17; 46:3).

According to Zechariah, one of the yearly feasts that all nations must attend when Messiah rules is the Feast of Tabernacles:

> *"And it shall come to pass that everyone who is left of all the nations which came against Jerusalem shall go up from year to year to worship the King, the LORD of hosts, and to keep the Feast of Tabernacles. And it shall be that whichever of the families of the earth do not come up to Jerusalem to worship the King, the LORD of hosts, on them there will be no rain."*
>
> – Zechariah 14:16-18 (NKJV)

The priestly rituals during the Feast of Tabernacles are connected to asking God for rain in the coming months. This rain theme continues during the millennial reign. Zechariah points out that, if the people from any nation refuse to attend the ceremonies and joyful celebrations of Tabernacles, then God will withhold the blessing of rain from their land:

> *"If the family of Egypt will not come up and enter in, they shall have no rain; they shall receive the plague with which the LORD strikes the nations who do not come up to keep the Feast of Tabernacles. This shall be the punishment of Egypt and the punishment of all the nations that do not come up to keep the Feast of Tabernacles."*
>
> – Zechariah 14:18-19 (NKJV)

The Feast of Tabernacles concludes a time known among devout Jews as the "seasons of our joy." Jewish beliefs about the days between Trumpets and the end of Tabernacles are as follows. On the Feast of Trumpets, the trumpet blasts a warning that the Day of Atonement is coming, in which God will determine judgment or mercy on His people. However, repentance is always followed by great joy and rejoicing, even in heaven where there is rejoicing over one sinner who repents (Luke 15:7). Following the Day of Atonement, the seven days of Tabernacles introduces the season of great celebration and rejoicing.

PREPARING THE LAND FOR THE MILLENNIAL REIGN

In the future, the Feast of Tabernacles will be a yearly festival in which the Messiah will blast the shofar, indicating that the season has come for all of Israel and the Gentile nations to ascend to Jerusalem for a celebration. Today, among devout Jews, Tabernacles is the only feast of the seven Biblical feasts where both Jews and Gentiles together participate in the rejoicing. Today during Feast of Tabernacles, modern Israel is filled with tens of thousands of tourists from around the world who arrive to spend several days in the Holy Land with other Jewish believers. Imagine, during the millennial reign of Christ, the multitudes that will cover the mountains surrounding Jerusalem during the Tabernacles festival!

Many years ago I stood in the Judean Wilderness and pondered the Biblical predictions which indicated that entire nations will travel to Jerusalem and attend the Feast of Tabernacles. Jerusalem is in the land of Judea, and the tribal region of ancient Judea included the Judean Wilderness, which is approximately 579 square miles. It is mostly barren, with cliffs, rocks and plateaus. There is also the Negev desert, which covers 4,700 square miles. With this much desert, how could Israel provide food and water to entire nations of people who would ascend the mountains of Jerusalem to celebrate at a new Temple where the Messiah rules?

PREPARING THE LAND FOR THE REIGN OF THE KING

The prophet Isaiah reported 2,600 years ago that a miracle would occur in the heart of the deserts of Israel. The following prophecy might seem simple and insignificant, until the reader understands the large area the prediction effects and the miracle it involves. First, the prophecy:

> *"The wilderness and the solitary place shall be glad for them; and the desert shall rejoice, and blossom as the rose. It shall blossom abundantly, and rejoice even with joy and singing: the glory of Lebanon shall be*

given unto it, the excellency of Carmel and Sharon, they shall see the glory of the LORD, and the excellency of our God.

Strengthen ye the weak hands, and confirm the feeble knees. Say to them that are of a fearful heart, be strong, fear not: behold, your God will come with vengeance, even God with a recompense; he will come and save you.

Then the eyes of the blind shall be opened, and the ears of the deaf shall be unstopped. Then shall the lame man leap as an hart, and the tongue of the dumb sing: for in the wilderness shall waters break out, and streams in the desert. And the parched ground shall become a pool, and the thirsty land springs of water: in the habitation of dragons, where each lay, shall be grass with reeds and rushes.

And a highway shall be there, and a way, and it shall be called The way of holiness; the unclean shall not pass over it; but it shall be for those: the wayfaring men, though fools, shall not err therein. No lion shall be there, nor any ravenous beast shall go up thereon, it shall not be found there; but the redeemed shall walk there: And the ransomed of the LORD shall return, and come to Zion with songs and everlasting joy upon their heads: they shall obtain joy and gladness, and sorrow and sighing shall flee away."

– Isaiah 35:1-10

A HEBREW WORD STUDY

When reading the English translation of the Bible, the words *desert* or *wilderness* indicate no specific location. To us in the west, the word desert brings to mind a large, sandy or rocky desert, or a barren or desolate area with sand and cactus. In the original Hebrew, however, there are numerous words that identify a specific location within Israel, from the border of Egypt in the south, toward the north near the Sea of Galilee.

For example, Israel crossed the Red Sea and entered the wilderness of *Sin*, a stretch of wilderness between Elim and Mount Sinai (Exod. 16:1). During their journey, the second area Israel encountered was the desert surrounding the *Sinai*, which according to Paul in Galatians is located in Arabia (Exod. 19:1; Gal. 4:25). A region not mentioned by its present name in the English Bible is the Negev desert, a large stretch between Egypt and Israel. In Jeremiah 2:6 the word used for *wilderness* is the Hebrew word *midbar*. Looking at Deuteronomy 32:10, Moses is describing the wilderness and uses another Hebrew word, *Y'shemon* meaning a place without vegetation.

In Isaiah's prophecy, two important Hebrew words are keys to identifying the area where this prediction will come to pass. The word *wilderness* in Isaiah 35:1 is *tizar*. But the most important word in this passage is the Hebrew word for desert. This word is the Hebrew word *Aravah*. Literally, the prophet is saying, *"The Tizar will be glad and the Aravah will blossom as a rose."*

THE ARAVAH MIRACLE

In Israel, there are two areas classified as the Aravah. The first is the African-Syrian rift that runs south from the Sea of Galilee and ends at the northern part of the Dead Sea. It also runs parallel on either side of the Jordan River. The Aravah region that many believe Isaiah was referring to is south of the Dead Sea, and stretches for approximately 120 miles directly south, ending at the Gulf of Aquaba.

From the beginning of civilization, this region has been considered some of the most barren and desolate land in the Holy Land. It consists of a dry mixture of sand, dirt and rock. When traveling south from the Dead Sea, one can see an occasional desert bush or an Acacia tree, known for surviving in dry, desert regions. Since the beginning of known history, no vegetation has grown in this area, nor do you find many people living there.

Years ago a satellite picture identified a large underground water source in the heart of the Aravah. Israelis began drilling underground and discovered a huge lake of underground water! Using this water source, the agriculturists began to install water pumps and irrigation pipes throughout the desert, initiating a farming project that today is nothing less than astonishing.

I have traveled to this region on numerous occasions to document the miracle in the desert. In 1985, I stood on Mount Nebo in Jordan and looked over into Israel to the northern Aravah rift, where Jericho is located. There was only one large green patch surrounding the palm oasis of Jericho. Today there seem to be tens of thousands of acres of farms stretching from the Sea of Galilee to the northern part of the Dead Sea. In the southern half of the Aravah, below the Dead Sea, there are now at least fifty-four farms spread throughout the Negev and Aravah, and they produce tomatoes, peppers, melons, and many other foods.

I once visited a farm that produces 100-120 kilotons of tomatoes per acre, while America produces about 20-30 pounds per acre. Even the cows in the region give more milk, up to 4,000 gallons a year compared to the average American cow that gives 2,500 gallons a year. This in an area, that for 5,800 years, was a barren wasteland, and the land which the prophet saw blossoming.

MORE DETAILS REVEALED

There is more to this prophecy than just the fact the Aravah is blossoming. Isaiah saw a pool of water in the desert. A large pool exists in the desert this day and has been named Sapphire for its deep blue color. This water is coming from underneath the desert and the total amount of underground water is over fifty times that of all the fresh water in Israel. The prophet said there would be grass, reeds and rushes in the area of the pool. At this location, there are presently grass, reeds and rushes surrounding the pool of water. The prophet also predicted there would be springs of water, and that "waters shall break out and springs in the desert" (Isa. 41:18; 49:10).

That passage literally came alive to me years ago when I traveled to the lower Aravah. I observed that water was flowing from the top of a hill and emptying into the beautiful pool of bluish water. Underground pressure had forced the water upward through small cracks in the ground, and miniature springs of water were pushing up from out of the ground surrounding the pool. In fact, the rocks were being split as the water pushed through the cracks, reminding me of when Moses smote the rock in the desert and water gushed out for the people to drink (Exod. 17:6). This water was being diverted through several man-made channels layered with rocks and cement, into the pool below.

Another point of interest is the statement that the glory of Carmel would be given to the area. Mount Carmel is a beautiful mountain range that runs for about thirteen miles along the edge of the Jezreel Valley. The name Carmel in Hebrew means, "God's vineyard," as the mountain is noted for its trees—including fruit trees and vineyards. Today, one of the leading packing companies in Israel that ships food and vegetables from Israel throughout the world is the Carmel Packing Company. The glory of Carmel indicates that the blessing of productivity given to Mount Carmel will also be given to the desert.

The prophecy also indicates that a road will pass through the Aravah. Today there is a large paved road passing directly beside this pool of water and continuing near the farms in this area. It is the main road coming from Eilat in the south and heading northward to the Dead Sea. The prophets spoke of Egypt coming to Jerusalem to worship the Lord, and for this to occur roads must exist and food must be available. I believe that during the one-thousand-year (millennial) reign of Christ, this road will be filled with travelers who will come from the Northern horn of Africa up to Jerusalem to worship the Lord. The farms will be thriving with delicious food as pilgrims head to the Holy City during the Feast of Tabernacles (Zech. 14:16).

Roads will link the surrounding nations with Israel, and one such road is mentioned by Isaiah:

"In that day shall there be a highway out of Egypt to Assyria, and the Assyrian shall come into Egypt, and the Egyptian into Assyria, and the Egyptians shall serve with the Assyrians. In that day shall Israel be the third with Egypt and with Assyria, even a blessing in the midst of the land."

– ISAIAH 19:23-24

Yet another prophecy is presently being fulfilled. For several years, Israel has used massive equipment to drill through mountains to prepare roads and tunnels, thus providing ways to travel into the West Bank underground and bypass the other roads in and out of Arab villages. These roads are like a super highway and will, in the future, provide the means for nations to travel to Jerusalem. The roads are being prepared, but what about the need for massive food supplies?

THE PROPHECY OF THE FRUIT

Isaiah not only saw Israel return to the land, he predicted that their agricultural blessings would also be a blessing to the world:

"He shall cause them that come of Jacob to take root: Israel shall blossom and bud, and fill the face of the world with fruit."

— ISAIAH 27:6

The Hebrew prophets predicted that the Jews would return to Israel from Gentile nations and take root in the last days. This Hebrew phrase, to take root, means *to strike the soil*. It can allude to the people of the land striking the soil in order to pluck something from it. As the people take root, the land will be blessed and, according to Isaiah, Israel will become a major exporter of fruit. The Hebrew word for fruit is *tunavah,* and it means crops. Israel is an exporter of all types of food, and the nation produces ninety-five percent of its own food requirements. At last count Israel now has over 725 agricultural communities.

The miracle of the blossoming of the desert is considered a sign of both God's favor on the land and the soon appearing of the Messiah. Even Christian scholars identified this miracle with the return of the Lord, specifically when Christ would reign for a thousand years from Jerusalem. In the 1940s, Mr. Finis Dake, author of the popular *Dake's Annotated Reference Bible,* commented on Isaiah 35 regarding the desert blossoming. He said:

> "The time of the fulfillment will be the millennium, for none of these things are being accomplished today in some spiritual way of life, and this also indicates a literal meaning of every prediction…" (Dake's Bible, Page 706, section b note 12)

In the 1940s when Dake wrote this commentary, Israel was not a nation. Mr. Dake interpreted the time of Isaiah's fulfillment to be the thousand-year reign of Christ. If this prediction was believed by earlier scholars to occur when the Messiah returns to reign, and the prophecy is presently being fulfilled in full or in part, then this should be a sign of Christ's soon return. God is presently preparing the physical land of Israel for the return of Christ. Multitudes of saints and people living on the earth will conduct pilgrimages to the Holy City each year to rejoice in the Torah, who will be Christ, instead of words penned on a kosher scroll.

The southern Aravah connects Egypt and northern Africa with Israel, and the northern Aravah runs parallel to the west side of the Jordan River and to the nation of Jordan. The northern farms can provide the food for those coming from the countries north of Jerusalem, such as Lebanon and Syria. The blossoming of the desert is considered in Scripture and in rabbinical literature to be a prophetic sign that occurs at the end of the age, near the time the Messiah returns. The land of Israel is being prepared in advance for the rule of Christ.

RESURRECTION AND TABERNACLES

The New Testament may reveal one more prophetic clue within the Feast of Tabernacles. Matthew records the transfiguration of Christ in Matthew 17. During this event, Moses and Elijah appeared, to the astonishment of Peter, James and John. In his zeal, Peter suggested, "Lord, it is good for us to be here: if thou wilt, let us make here three tabernacles; one for thee, and one for Moses, and one for Elias" (Matt. 17:4).

Herein we find an interesting clue. In John 7:2, the apostle records that Christ was in Jerusalem at the Feast of Tabernacles. During this season, Jews would build a booth and spend time outdoors as a reminder that their forefathers dwelt in tents in the wilderness. The Greek word for tabernacles in both instances is *skene*, which refers to a tent or hut. Why would Peter suggest building three tabernacles?

It is suggested that the transfiguration occurred during the time of the Feast of Tabernacles, which in the context makes sense. If it were not on the feast, the imagery paints the picture of the future millennial kingdom. Christ is transfigured, and the Greek word is *metamorphoo*, which is derived from two words: *meta*, which carries the idea of *exchange*, and the word *morphoo*, which means to *change a person's outward form*. The combined words mean to change a person's outward form. Paul wrote that those living at Christ's return would be "changed in the moment, in the twinkling of an eye" (1 Cor. 15:51).

Paul used the word *allasso* for *changed*, meaning to be made different. The change will occur when our corruptible body puts on incorruption, and this mortal body puts on immortality (1 Cor. 15:53).

Not only was Christ transformed in His body for a brief time, but Elijah and Moses were present. Moses represented the law and Elijah the prophets. Moses had died fifteen hundred years prior, and God Himself buried him in the plains of Moab (Deut. 34:6). Moses had not been resurrected yet, but it was his spirit and soul which appeared on the mountain. Elijah, however, was caught up alive to heaven (2 Kings 2), and thus he, too, was seen by Christ and the three Apostles.

The imagery is clear. Elijah represents those who will be living at the return of Christ, and Moses represents those who will have died at Christ's coming; yet both will be changed and transformed at the coming of Christ (1 Thess. 4:16-17; 1 Cor. 15: 52-54). Peter suggested three tabernacles. There was an early idea that this feast represented the resurrection of the dead and the kingdom of the Messiah.

Methodius, one of the church fathers who passed in AD 311, gave an explanation of the Feast of Tabernacles and its connection to the millennial reign:

> "For they only who have celebrated the Feast of Tabernacles come to the Holy Land, setting out from those dwellings which are called tabernacles, until they come to enter into the temple and city of God, advancing to a greater and more glorious joy, as the Jewish types indicate. For I also, taking my journey and going forth from Egypt of this life, come first to the resurrection which is the true Feast of Tabernacles, and having set up my tabernacle, adorned with the fruits of virtue, on the first day of the resurrection, which is the day of judgment, celebrate with Christ the Millennium of rest, which is called the seventh day, even the true Sabbath" (253-4).

Peter, James and John had been sleeping prior to the moment of the transfiguration. When they suddenly awoke, Peter began shouting about building three tabernacles—one for Christ, one for Moses, and the third for Elijah. It appears he assumed that both Moses and Elijah had now arrived on earth and, with Jesus glowing in white, perhaps

Peter thought the resurrection and kingdom had now arrived. His assumption was that Jesus, Elijah and Moses were now preparing to set up the kingdom. Peter's imagery was correct, in that Tabernacles was themed with resurrection and kingdom, but his timing was certainly wrong.

There will be several orders of resurrection in the future that must be distinguished from the general resurrection of the dead in Christ at the Rapture. Those who have passed when the great gathering together occurs will be resurrected (1 Thess. 4:16-17). In the book of Revelation, we see the two witnesses killed and resurrected after three and one half days (Rev. 11:7-9).

At the conclusion of the seven-year tribulation, there is another resurrection of those who died during the tribulation who will be raised with Christ to rule for a thousand years (Rev. 20:4). These are the same individuals that Daniel spoke about who would arise from the dust (Dan. 12:2) after the time of trouble (Dan. 12:1), which is a reference to the end of the great tribulation.

Through this study we see that Passover is our redemption, Pentecost is our Holy Spirit baptism, and Tabernacles is our resurrection and rejoicing in the Messiah's kingdom.

CHAPTER 8

THE HANUKKAH CODE AND THE CLEANSING OF YOUR TEMPLE

T HERE ARE TWO yearly celebrations for devout Jews that are not a part of the Torah Feasts established by the Lord. However, the events surrounding these two unique times of Jewish history have been handed down for generations, memorialized, and celebrated as two of the greatest seasons of deliverance from their enemies. One is Purim, the celebration linked to the story of Queen Esther in Persia (see the book of Esther), and the other is called Chanukah, or Hanukkah, also called by some the "festival of lights." Both are considered minor Jewish holidays.

This section will show that Christ celebrated Hanukkah, and it will reveal the parallels between the cleansing of the Temple in Jerusalem and the necessity for each Believer to cleanse and sanctify their own mind and body, which is the temple of the Holy Spirit.

Hanukkah, or *dedication*, is a minor Jewish holiday inspired by a significant historical event. Derived from the Hebrew verb *hanak*, which means *to dedicate*, Hanukkah—or the Feast of Dedication—commemorates the rededication of the Temple in Jerusalem by Judah Maccabee in 165 BC after defeating the armies of Antiochus IV Epiphanes, king of Syria and oppressor of Israel. Because of this great triumph over the Greek invaders, Hanukkah—although a minor festival—is considered second only to Passover in historical significance. And so, like Passover, it is known as a feast of liberation.

Though it is not recorded for us in Scripture, the story of Hanukkah is well documented in the apocryphal text, 1 Maccabees, as well as the writings of Flavius Josephus. According to these accounts, Antiochus IV Epiphanes (Epiphanes being a title translated as "the risen god") was determined to stamp out the religion of the Jews and their faith in one God. He made it punishable by death to observe Shabbat, obey *kashrut* (dietary laws), or study the Torah. On 25 Kislev 168 BC, the Holy Temple in Jerusalem was designated as a center of worship for Zeus by order of Antiochus. He erected an image of Zeus beside the Altar of Sacrifice and, in an act of great insult to Jewish sensibilities, a pig was offered to Zeus on the altar.

Soon after these offensive activities occurred, a man from the priestly line named Mattityahu initiated a resistance in the small village of Modi'in. Upon his death, his son Judah continued the resistance under the banner, *Mi Kamocha b'elim YHVH,* meaning, "Who is like the LORD among the gods." The first Hebrew letter in each of these words formed the acrostic *Maccabi,* thus Judah and his followers became known as the Maccabees. Against overwhelming odds, Judah Maccabee (a word that also means "hammer") recaptured Jerusalem from the Greek armies.

When Judah and his followers entered the Temple compound, they found that three years of desolation had left God's House desecrated and in disarray. The gates were destroyed, weeds were growing in the courtyards, and garbage littered its buildings. The Jews immediately began to rid the Holy Place of these things. After smashing the idol of Zeus, the Maccabeans cleared the Temple courts of all the weeds and debris and then cleansed the Temple itself of all the litter. Included in this purification process was the dismantling of the altar that had been used to sacrifice to Zeus and replacing it with a new one.

On the 25th of Kislev, which was three years to the day since Temple services had been interrupted, Judah the Maccabee rededicated the Temple on Mt. Moriah. He lit the lamps of the great Menorah, offered incense on the Golden Altar, placed the showbread upon the

Table and offered burnt offerings upon the Altar of Sacrifice. In commemoration, Judah decreed that on the same day every year thereafter, the Jews were to celebrate Hanukkah for eight successive days. They were to kindle lights nightly during this period as soon as the first stars appeared, adding a new light to the others each night of the festival. This is why Hanukkah is also known as the Festival of Lights (see Josephus, Antiquities of the Jews, Book XII, chap. 7, sect. vi – vii & 1 Maccabees 3-4).

Besides recounting the story of Hanukkah, Jewish commentary gives a reason for why Judah ordained that the festival was to last over an eight day period. According to the *Mishna* (*Megillat Ta'anit 9*), it took eight days for the Maccabees to reconstruct the Altar of Sacrifice and, therefore, the celebration was to last eight days. However, according to the *Talmud* (Shabbat 21b), the reason is tied to a legend that describes a great miracle. The commentary states that, "when the Hasmoneans prevailed against the Greeks, they made search in the Temple and found only one jar of oil, which stood there untouched and undefiled, with the seal of the High Priest. It contained sufficient oil for one day's lighting only. But a miracle was wrought therein and they lit the lamps with it for eight days." Supposedly, this miracle allowed them time to prepare new oil for the menorah, a process that would have taken seven to eight days.

Many Christians who casually read the New Testament are unaware that Christ Himself was present in Jerusalem during Hanukkah. We read, in John 10:22-23, *"And it was at Jerusalem the feast of the dedication, and it was winter. And Jesus walked in the temple in Solomon's porch."* Solomon's porch was on the eastern side of the Temple to the left of the inside of the Eastern gate. The King James uses the term, "feast of dedication," which was another name commemorating the rededication of the Temple under the Maccabees.

THE CELEBRATION TODAY

Two thousand years later, Jews continue to remember this miracle and the rededication of the Temple by kindling the lights of Hanukkah. Beginning on the 25th day of Kislev on the Hebrew calendar (corresponding, approximately, to mid-December on the Gregorian calendar) and for eight successive nights, celebrants light a *chanukiyah* (a special nine-branched menorah), adding a new light each night. Many Jewish homes host feasts for friends and family complete with music, dancing and special foods. Typically, potato latkes (pancakes) and sufganiyot (doughnuts) are features of these gatherings because these foods are fried in oil, which is to recall the miracle of the oil that burned for eight days.

It is also customary to give children gifts of Hanukkah gelt (coins) that they may use in a game played with a four-sided spinning top called a dreidel. On each of the four sides of the dreidel are four different Hebrew letters—**n**un, **g**imel, **h**ei and **sh**iyn. These letters form an acrostic for the phrase *nes gadol hayah sham*, meaning, a great miracle happened there. The objective of the Hanukkah game is to parlay one's gelt into even more gelt. The outcome is determined by what Hebrew letter comes up when you spin the dreidel.

Traditionally this game recalls that, in the days of Antiochus, the Jews used the four-sided dreidel as a way of disguising their meetings to discuss the Torah—an act that was punishable by death. If any Greek investigated their assembly, it would appear that these men were simply engaging in a game of chance. So in many ways, Hanukkah is to Jews what Christmas is to Christians—a time for family to gather in a joyous, light-filled environment and to remember that the true reason for the celebration is deliverance from oppression. The lights of Hanukkah demonstrate that God enables something pure, however small it may seem, to give light well beyond its natural potential.

HANUKKAH'S SIGNIFICANCE FOR BELIEVERS

This festival is relevant to believers on many levels; yet, many Christians are not familiar with it. This is ironic considering that the only mention of this holiday in canonized Scripture is found in the New Testament. John's Gospel records that Jesus was in Jerusalem during the Feast of Dedication (Jn. 10:22-23) meaning He was there, presumably, to participate in the celebration of Hanukkah. Furthermore, to believers with a background in Judaism, the imagery is rich. Because Hanukkah begins on the 25th of Kislev and usually falls in December, many believers see a link between Hanukkah and the birth of Christ celebrated on December 25. Consider that Hanukkah is associated with the rededication of an earthly building, and the birth of Christ is the manifestation of the Living Temple of God. Jesus said of Himself, "Destroy this temple and in three days, I will raise it up" (Jn. 2:19). Although there are many other reasons for December 25 being recognized as the day of Christ's birth, perhaps the connection between 25 Kislev and December 25—the Roman calendar's equivalent—plays a role in that determination as well.

It is possible that December 25, or at least that time of year, may have a connection to the birth of Christ, but perhaps not in the way most people think. It is very likely that, instead of marking His birth, it is possibly the season when Mary was visited by the angel and when she, shortly thereafter, conceived by the Holy Spirit. In other words, her conception may have taken place at or around the time of Hanukkah which begins on 25 Kislev.

This is especially noteworthy because, for centuries, Jewish mystics have argued that the Hanukkah lights should be seen, ultimately, as a hidden manifestation of the Messiah. If Mary was visited at this time of year, this would put the birth of Christ around the time of *Yom Teruah* (Feast of Trumpets) also known as *Rosh HaShanah (*literally, "head of the year"), or possibly the Feast of Tabernacles.

It is interesting that Hanukkah and Christmas come just before the Gregorian calendar's New Year because, on a spiritual level, Hanukkah is equivalent to Rosh HaShanah. The Jewish New Year offers an opportunity to part with the past and begin a new season, spiritually renewed. Hanukkah, with its imagery of cleansing the Temple, rekindling the lights of the Menorah, and the rededication of the altar also offers one an opportunity to be spiritually renewed. As a Christian, it is easy to see how Christ is revealed in the themes of both holidays but, in particular, Hanukkah.

Cleansing the Temple of filth and rededicating a pure Temple is the true story of Hanukkah and, as believers, we are to understand that our bodies are temples of the Holy Spirit (1 Corinthians 3:16).

That Christ was most likely conceived during Hanukkah and birthed at Rosh HaShanah—two holidays connected by common themes of cleansing and spiritual renewal—illustrates that the incarnation of the Messiah is what makes it possible for us, God's earthly temples, to be cleansed, rededicated and transformed into new creatures. This theme is why we suggest that rededication is, in fact, a more fitting definition of Hanukkah. This holiday is a time to remove the carnal debris from our lives, to rekindle within us the light of God's presence, and to rededicate ourselves to the true worship of God. The fact that God became flesh and dwelt among us makes this transformation from a defiled temple to a pure one possible.

Rabbis have noted that the word Hanukkah can be divided into two smaller words: *heno*, meaning "His grace," and *kah*, which is numerically equivalent to 25. It is said that this illustrates Hanukkah's association with the light of Creation. Traditionally, Rosh HaShanah (1st day of the Hebrew month Tishri) was the day that Adam was created, the sixth day of Creation. This means that the first day of Creation, when God said, "Let there be light," would have been the 25th day of the month Elul. Thus, the *kah* of Hanukkah (numerically equivalent to 25) is associated with the light of Creation, also known as the Light of the World. Through that light we can see and, thus, comprehend *heno*—His grace. We see that His grace appeared at the very beginning of Creation, in conjunction with the Light of the World, to illuminate our hearts and change our lives. Christ, of course, is the Light of the World and the personification of His grace.

As noted before, during Hanukkah, children play a game with a dreidel upon which are found the Hebrew letters **nun, gimel, hei** and **shiyn**, forming an acrostic for the phrase *nes gadol hayah sham.* However, it has also been noted in rabbinical literature that this acrostic can also be rendered as **nefesh** (soul), **guf** (body), **sekhel** (intellect or mind), **hakol** (all of the above joined together). The numerical value or gematria of these four letters totals 358, equivalent to the value of the Hebrew word *Mashiach* or *Messiah* (**mem, shiyn, yud** and **chet**). Therefore, it has long been understood that the dreidel game—which was developed by the need to secretly discuss the Scriptures under the watchful eye of the oppressor—ultimately reveals the Messiah, and that He alone is authorized to renew us completely—soul, mind and body. Only He can perform "a great miracle" in our lives and enable us to rededicate ourselves to loving the LORD our God with all our heart, mind and strength.

There is a saying used at Hanukkah: *madlikin shemonah yemei Hanukkah* which means, "We light eight days of Hanukkah." In Hebrew, the first letters of these four words are *mem, shin, yud and chet*. These letters spell the Hebrew word *Mashiach*, again illustrating that Messiah is indeed hidden within the lights of Hanukkah. In fact, one Jewish commentator, speaking of the Messiah says, "Whose coming we hasten by this act [lighting the Hanukkah lights]." For hundreds of years, Jewish mystics have regarded the Hanukkah lights as a manifestation of the hidden light of the Messiah.

So then, to preserve the tradition of kindling these special lights, Judaism developed a nine-branched menorah (*chanukiyah*). Eight of these branches represent the eight days of Hanukkah. The additional branch, which typically stands above the other eight branches, is called the *shammash* or servant. This is the first lamp kindled each night and the one from which the light is extended to all of the other branches on their appointed days. Thus, the shammash branch *serves* the others by giving them light.

This branch is reminiscent of the main or central branch of the seven-branched menorah that stood in the Holy Place. That particular branch represented the *ner tamid* or "eternal light," for the light of the Menorah was never to be extinguished. Consequently, the Hanukkah shammash represents the eternal light or "light of the world" which serves to give light to the other branches of the chanukiyah.

There is a tradition in Judaism that suggests the seven-branched menorah was detailed on each of its branches with the twenty-two letters of the Hebrew alphabet. On the middle branch—the one corresponding with the shammash—were the letters **y**ud, **k**af, **l**amed and **m**em. These four letters read as a word are *y'khalem* which means "He makes them whole or complete." This is interesting because, when Jesus appeared to John on the isle of Patmos, He stood in the midst of the seven golden candlesticks or *menorot* (Rev. 1:13). It is very possible that Jesus stood in the position of the central branch, thus corresponding with the branch representing the eternal light, and the one also known as the shammash or servant. In this we see that Messiah is the one who cleanses the filth from within our temple and makes us whole.

These same four letters read in reverse form the Hebrew word *malkhi* which means "my King" and so we see that the King came to earth to be a servant. The Light of the Word came to be a light to all and to free us from oppression and slavery. He enabled us to rid our lives of the garbage that cluttered our hearts. Through His sacrifice we can now present our bodies as a living sacrifice and transform our being into a holy habitation for the Most High God.

Hanukkah serves as a reminder to Christians as well as Jews that, as God's people, we are to dedicate ourselves to His service. In so doing, we allow His light in us to shine for the whole world to see so that, as Isaiah prophesied, His glory will be seen upon us and "the nations shall come to your light" (Isa. 60:2-3).

Just as it was necessary to purge the defilement at the Jewish Temple, we are to sanctify and cleanse ourselves from the filthiness of the flesh and spirit (2 Cor. 7:1). Thus, because we are a temple of the Holy Spirit (1 Cor. 3:16-17), Hanukkah speaks to us of the importance of maintaining holiness and purity in our body, soul, and spirit.

CHAPTER 9

THE PURIM CODE
IN ESTHER

*"On the thirteenth day of the month Adar; and
on the fourteenth day of the same rested they,
and made it a day of feasting and gladness."*

— ESTHER 9:17

D EVOUT JEWS AND many Christians are fully aware of the seven
appointed feasts, their meanings, and the prophetic applications. But some Christians might not be familiar with the
lesser known cycles or special seasons that were established by God.
The Sabbath cycles were weekly (every seventh day), yearly (every seventh year) and every forty-nine years (seven years times seven). Israel's months were determined after the first sliver of the new moon
appeared. New moon offerings were given at the Temple each month.
The third appointed season was Jubilee.

The two non-Torah celebrations recognized to this day among
devout Jews are Hanukah and Purim. The Torah emphasizes the first
(Nissan) and seventh month (Tishri) as the months for the seven yearly
festivals. On the Jewish calendar the twelfth month is Adar, and this
is the month when Purim is celebrated.

THE PURIM FACTOR

Purim, or "lots," a minor Jewish holiday, was inspired by a major historical event commemorating the deliverance of the Jews living in Persia in the 5th century BC. The miraculous deliverance was accomplished through Queen Esther (whose actual name was Hadassah) and her kinsman Mordechai. The Agagite Haman, viceroy to King Ahasuerus, had plotted to exterminate the Jews in all 127 Persian provinces—an area that stretched from Ethiopia to India. Having convinced Ahasuerus that the Jews were disloyal, he received the king's consent to follow through with his plan. Haman's order stated that lots were to be drawn to determine the day on which the massacre was to occur. The date determined was the 13th of the Hebrew month Adar. According to the Bible, his diabolical plot was frustrated when Esther, warned by Mordechai, developed a plan of her own. Ignoring the potential danger she faced, Esther boldly approached the king unannounced and made a successful appeal to have the murderous decree annulled. Consequently, the Jews of Persia were permitted to defend themselves against their enemies and did so on the 14th day of Adar; and in Shushan, the Persian capital, the attack on Haman's followers continued for one more day.

As for the evil instigator Haman, his position of authority was taken from him and given to the righteous Mordechai (Est. 8:2). Haman was then hung upon the very gallows he had constructed for Mordechai's execution (Esther 7:10). In the end, the destruction that had been meant for the Jews was reversed and visited upon those who hated them. To commemorate this great deliverance, Mordechai declared that Jews should always celebrate Purim with feasting, gladness, and giving of gifts in acknowledgment that their sorrow was turned to joy (Est. 9:22).

HOW PURIM IS CELEBRATED TODAY

Mordechai's decree to celebrate Purim is still being honored today by Jews around the world. In Jewish communities, Purim is indeed a day of feasting, gift giving, and joyous celebration.

Before the festivities begin, the day before—the 13th of Adar—is observed with fasting. It is called *Ta'anit Esther* or the "Fast of Esther," in remembrance of the young Jewish girl who became the Queen of Persia and who risked her life in order to deliver her people. It also commemorates the fact that Persia's Jews joined with her in this fast as she prepared to approach King Ahasuerus unannounced—an act that was punishable by death. On this fast day, Jews observe the custom of *mishloach manot;* that is, the sending of gifts to friends and family as indicated in the book of Esther (9:22). These gifts consist of money, food, and delicacies as an expression of joy in Haman's defeat.

On the day of Purim—the 14th of Adar—celebrants congregate in their synagogues and read the *Megillat Esther* (scroll of Esther) to remember the miraculous story of deliverance. During the reading, each time Mordechai's name is mentioned, everyone will whistle and shout, "Hurrah." When the name of Haman is mentioned, people stamp their feet, clap their hands, or use various noisemakers called *groggers* to drown out the sound of his name. This is done to express that his name is being "erased" from the Megillat (the scroll of Esther). A verse in Exodus 17:14 is often quoted in connection with this tradition: "For I will utterly blot out the remembrance of Amalek from under heaven" (Deut. 25:19). This is cited because Haman's ancestors were not Persian but Amalekites.

After the reading of Esther's scroll, a great feast is held on the afternoon of the holiday. Traditional foods such as *kreplach* and *hamantaschen* are eaten to remind one of the particulars of the Purim story. For instance, *hamantaschen*—a German word that means "Haman's pockets"—are triangular shaped pastries filled with fruit or cheese that are intended to remind us that the wicked Haman filled his pockets with bribes. Another tradition has it that the triangular shape mimics the type of hat Haman was thought to have worn. The *challah* (specialty bread) made for Purim has particularly long braids to represent the long ropes that were used to hang Haman and his sons.

Tradition and custom aside, the primary focus of the holiday's festivities is this: Israel's enemies plotted to destroy them, but their enemies were destroyed instead. In Jewish communities outside of Jerusalem, the celebration of Purim is observed on the 14th of Adar. But because

Jerusalem is considered a walled city, the holiday is observed on the following day known as *Shushan Purim* (15th of Adar). The reason for this is due to the distinction between walled and unwalled cities made in the book of Esther. The attack of the Jews against their enemies concluded in Persia's capital, Shushan (a walled city), on the 15th of Adar; thus, all walled cities were to observe the holiday on this same date.

PURIM'S SIGNIFICANCE FOR BELIEVERS

Unlike Passover, Pentecost, and the Feast of Tabernacles, the celebration of Purim is not mandated by God's decree. However, it is impossible for attentive Bible students to ignore the incredible spiritual importance of this special holiday. It is one of the greatest examples in Scripture of how God does indeed "curse him who curses you" (Gen. 12:3) and repays the nations that are militarily aggressive toward Israel with the very sentence of destruction they intend to impose upon God's people.

This Purim principle does not end with the events recorded in Esther, but repeats itself time and again. Two noteworthy instances in modern history are the two Gulf Wars. The first Gulf War was initiated by Saddam Hussein's invasion of Kuwait in 1990. Being threatened with invasion himself, he quickly turned his Scud missiles on the citizens of Israel. Soon after, missiles and bombs began falling on Saddam Hussein and his armies, culminating in his surrender—on Purim (14th of Adar)!

Twelve years later, the second Gulf War began and resulted in the complete capitulation of Saddam Hussein's regime and the elimination of one of Israel's most aggressive enemies. That particular war began on Shushan Purim (15th of Adar). It is interesting that Saddam Hussein bragged that he could defeat Israel, and his final defeat would be initiated at the season of Purim. It is also prophetic that, just as Haman was hung on the gallows, Saddam met his death by hanging!

Because of this recurring phenomenon, Purim is viewed by some as a minor Yom Kippur. In fact, the Hebrew spelling of *yom ha'kippurim* (Day of Atonement) can also be rendered as "a day like purim." It was on Yom Kippur that lots were drawn to see which sacrifice would be offered unto God and which would be released into the wilderness. More importantly, in Judaism it is believed that on the Day of Atonement, all the accusations railed against Israel by the adversary are silenced.

One factor supporting this view is that the Hebrew letters of *ha'satan* (literally, the adversary) has a gematria (a numerical value) of 364—one day short of 365, the number of days in a solar year. Thus the accuser, ha'satan, hurls accusations at Israel throughout the year; but on Yom Kippur, he is commanded to keep silent. On that day, the source of his accusations—sin—is covered by the blood of the sacrificial gift. This reversal of fortune echoes the story of Purim: Haman's false accusations of disloyalty were silenced when the accuser of Israel was taken to the gallows.

This story recorded in the book of Esther is particularly interesting because, of all the books in the Bible, Esther is the only one that does not mention the name of God. Judaism concludes that this is because the book was originally a scroll sent in the form of a letter. Therefore, the name of God was omitted by the writers for fear that the letter might be desecrated or mishandled in some way, thus failing to show the proper respect for the ineffable name of God, YHVH. This certainly sounds reasonable in a practical way, but might it also be possible that this book is a prime example of how God chooses to conceal Himself in the affairs of the world, being discernible only to those who are looking for Him?

Jesus stated that some people were given the privilege of understanding the mystery of the kingdom of God; but to those who are outside, all things come in parables (Mark 4:11). Christ based this statement on a prophecy in Isaiah 6:9-10 which refers to people who hear but do not understand, who see but do not perceive. Their lack of perception is not determined by God's unwillingness to reveal His truth; but it is due to their unwillingness to seek after His truth with their whole heart. Christ said, *"Seek and you will find; knock and it will be opened to you; for everyone who asks receives, and he who seeks finds, and to him who knocks it will be opened."* (Matt. 7:7-8). Those who seek to understand the mystery of the Kingdom of God will be shown His truth, but those who do not seek will not. He reveals Himself to those who seek for Him, and He conceals Himself from those who do not wish to look for Him.

Proverbs 25:2 tells us, *"It is the glory of God to conceal a matter, but the glory of kings is to search out the matter."* In other words, God conceals things in order to provoke His people to look for those things. In this manner, He is glorified even more. We find this to be most evident in the Word of God, which is a fathomless treasure trove of knowledge for those committed to digging for it. Jesus said, *"Every scribe instructed concerning the kingdom of Heaven is like a householder who brings out of his treasure things new and old"* (Matt. 13:52). Again, the treasures God wishes to reveal will be made known only to those who diligently seek Him. In concealing Himself and that which He deems to be precious, He also guards what is holy from desecration and destruction at the hands of those who are profane and antagonistic toward His purposes. Christ said, *"Do not give what is holy to the dogs; nor cast your pearls before swine"* (Matt. 7:6). This clearly teaches us that those who are heathen and unclean will treat the holy things of God with disrespect; therefore, He hides things from them.

Consider Esther. When the king's decree to find a new wife was made known, Mordechai warned Hadassah (as she was known) not to reveal her Jewish ancestry (Esther 2:10). Thus, the young Benjamite girl became known as Esther. The name Esther is not of Hebrew origin, but is a name associated with the Babylonian fertility goddess Ishtar (also known as Astarte, Ashteroth, or Easter). It is striking that a virtuous Hebrew woman would be known by a name associated with a pagan goddess. Yet, the Hebrew spelling of Esther suggests something beyond the obvious: something has been hidden from the eyes of the heathen and is visible only to those who are looking for the handiwork of the Creator.

The four Hebrew letters that spell "Esther" can also be rendered as the Hebrew word *esater* which means, "I will conceal." Thus, God permits the Hebrew Hadassah to "masquerade" as the Persian Esther.

Why would God conceal the Hebrew Hadassah in the guise of the

Persian Esther? He alone knew the heart of the wicked Haman before the Agagite was ever elevated to the position that would allow him to persecute God's people. Thus, the Purim story demonstrates that, even though God is not mentioned by name, the Creator was already at work positioning and concealing one of His servants so that all of His people might be delivered. Even though His name is not written in the scroll of Esther, He nevertheless is glorified in the outcome.

This is such an important principle for believers to embrace. Even when we cannot perceive the Adversary's threat against us and our family, the heavenly Father is already working on our behalf. He simply wants us to commit ourselves to His purposes with our whole heart.

In the festival of Purim, we also learn the value of knowing why we have been placed in the position we have and the importance of functioning in that purpose, regardless of what it requires of us. Perhaps Esther wondered why such favor had been shown her by being chosen queen against such odds. In time, circumstances answered those questions, and we see that the favor she received was not entirely for her benefit, but for the well-being of an entire nation of people. We see that the favor extended to her required a deep commitment to a greater purpose, and the fortitude to see that purpose through, even if it meant putting her life on the line. Perhaps it seemed to her that the palace insulated her from the impending storm, but Mordechai provoked her to realize that all the good that had come to her was not for her good alone. He warned Esther that, if she did not use what Heaven had bestowed upon her for a righteous purpose, then another would arise in her place.

Mordechai was not asking Esther to act in a way that he was unwilling to do himself. It was Mordechai's refusal to bow down and worship Haman as a god that incited Haman's wrath against Mordechai and the Jews in the first place. Ironically, in Persia we find a descendant of Benjamin (Mordechai) resisting the intended tyranny of a descendant of Amalek (Haman). This is interesting because, centuries before, another descendant of Benjamin (King Saul) refused to put to death the king of the Amalekites (Agag) in defiance to God's command (1 Samuel 15:9). Consequently, the kingdom was taken from Saul and given to David.

The Amalekites were direct descendants of Esau who, according to Scripture, felt that Jacob had stolen his birthright and blessing, and thus determined to kill Jacob. However, Scripture also tells us that, according to God, the birthright and blessing rightfully belonged to Jacob (Genesis 25:23, Malachi 1:2-3). Therefore, the argument can be made that Mordechai, knowing that the God of Israel had decreed that Jacob (Israel) would rule over Esau (Amalek), refused to bow to someone who was destined to be under his feet. In so doing, he placed great trust in God and, by his actions, demonstrated incredible faith that God had orchestrated these events and would ultimately deliver His people.

Mordechai's call for Esther to act culminated in the words that every believer must take to heart: "perchance you have come into the kingdom for such a time as this" (Esther 4:14). Those words caused Esther to conclude that fasting and prayer were necessary, so that God's people might be delivered and she might have the courage to be His instrument of salvation. In her call to prayer and fasting, she also acknowledged a mindset that is prevalent in other saints who have placed everything on the line, for she says, "If I perish, I perish" (Esther 4:16).

This courageous declaration reminds us of another statement issued to King Nebuchadnezzar of Babylon by Shadrach, Meshech and Abednego. Having been previously exalted by the king to positions of influence, they subsequently found themselves in a situation that, like Esther, required them to break the king's law under the penalty of death. Nevertheless, they resolved that if death was the consequence of adhering to God's purposes, then so be it. They were committed to the purpose that had been given them and so they declared, *"God whom we serve is able to deliver us from the burning fiery furnace… But if not, let it be known to you O king, that we do not serve your gods nor will we worship the gold image which you have set up"* (Dan. 3:17-18).

It is imperative that believers in the last days embrace this mindset, because the saints at the end of days will overcome the enemy by the blood of the Lamb and the word of their testimony, and they will love not their lives to the death (Rev. 12:11). Though the three Hebrews and Esther had to be willing to face death to further the greater purpose, it was not required of them to die. The hidden reason for their trial was so that God might demonstrate His might and power through willing vessels who submit to His sovereignty. The three Hebrew men came from the flames unharmed and without the smell of smoke on their clothing. As Esther boldly approached the king's throne, instead of having her killed, King Ahasuerus bestowed unprecedented favor upon her, thus paving the way for Esther and her people to overcome their enemy.

When we realize that our Father's purposes surpass ours; when we submit our will to His will; and when we have confidence in His promises, then we can confidently approach the Throne of Grace and obtain divine mercy, deliverance, and victory over our adversary.

THE HAMAN CODE

One of the great codes concealed in the story of Esther involves Haman and his ten sons. Haman was from Persia, and today the fanatical leadership of the Persian nation of Iran continually speaks of the destruction of Israel and the Jews. Haman plotted to kill all the Jews, just as the future antichrist will set his mind to move toward Jerusalem where, under the inspiration of Satan himself, this treacherous world dictator will attempt to annihilate the Jewish people and Israel. Haman's ten sons were aligned with their father in this plot.

However, Haman and his sons were eventually exposed by the queen and hung on the very gallows intended for the Jews. The future antichrist will have the assistance of ten kings, identified as the ten toes on the metallic image of Nebuchadnezzar (Dan. 2) and the ten horns on the beast (Rev. 17:12, 16). The intercession of Queen Esther, wife of the King of Persia, was vital to rescue the Jews throughout the world.

While the church is often identified as the Body of Christ or the Bride of Christ, Christ will return to earth as a King, thus making his bride the queen. At the conclusion of the seven-year tribulation, the queen bride will return with her King (Rev. 19) and participate in defeating the beast kingdom—the antichrist and his ten kings, and rescue the remnant of Jews from the antichrist's planned annihilation.

In my book, *Breaking the Jewish Code*, I present a fascinating code that is concealed in the Hebrew text. Years ago, a Jewish scholar working at the Qumran caves in Israel pointed out to me the double reference found in the Hebrew text of Esther. Two important verses read:

> *"The ten sons of Haman the son of Hammedatha, the enemy of the Jews, slew they; but on the spoil laid they not their hand."*
>
> – Esther 9:10

> *"Then said Esther, If it please the king, let it be granted to the Jews which are in Shushan to do tomorrow also according unto this day's decree, and let Haman's ten sons be hanged upon the gallows."*
>
> – Esther 9:13

Esther 9:10 said the Jews slew Haman's ten sons. Three verses later it says that his ten sons were "hanged upon the gallows." Were they initially slain (v-10), and then their bodies placed on the gallows (v-13)? Why is the death of the ten sons mentioned twice? Or is this a double reference to a *literal* and *future* event? In the Esther story, Haman is a prophetic picture of the future antichrist of prophecy, and Haman's ten sons are a prophetic preview of the ten kings of the apocalypse who will arise and give their kingdom to the antichrist (Rev. 17:12-17). This is a prophetic layer hidden in the story. If, however, we dig deeper into the actual Hebrew text, there is another message within the text.

Below is a list of Haman's ten sons:

1. Parshandatha	6. Aridatha
2. Dalphon	7. Parmashta
3. Aspatha	8. Arisai
4. Portha	9. Adriai
5. Adalia	10. Vajezatha

In the Hebrew text, the first, seventh and tenth names of Haman's sons have one Hebrew letter in each name that is one half the sizes of the other Hebrew letters in the ten names. The three Hebrew letters are Tav, Shin, and Tzion. When adding up the number value of these three letters they total 5706, which on the Jewish calendar becomes the Gregorian calendar year of 1946. So 1946 was the Jewish year 5706.

On October 16, 1946 eleven Nazi's were scheduled to be hung for their war crimes against the Jews. Prior to the hanging, one Nazi named Herman Goring committed suicide, leaving ten. When these ten Nazis were hung, their deaths fell on Purim. The hanging of the Nazi war criminals fell on the Hebrew calendar on the 21st of Tishri which is the seventh day of the Feast of Tabernacles, also called Hosanna Rabbah, the "Day of the Final Verdict."

The three smaller Hebrew letters in the Hebrew scroll of Esther were not formed in modern times, but existed in that form and were copied in that manner for centuries. Yet, what some thought was a copyist mistake was actually a prophetic clue to a future event that would one day repeat the same events recorded in the story of Esther. Thus the Esther Code conceals a future event in a past story.

As Haman and his sons sought to destroy all of the Jews, so will the antichrist and his ten kings initiate a final attempt to destroy the Jewish people. However, just as Haman met his doom, the antichrist will meet his doom and the Jewish people will survive the tribulation, as did the Jews in the 127 provinces (Est. 1:1). Esther the queen ruled with the king, and the saints will rule with Christ for a thousand years (Rev. 20:1-6).

CHAPTER 10

THE PRIESTHOOD AND THE PATTERNS OF FIRST FRUITS

IN THE DAYS of the Temple in Jerusalem, there were seven types of grains and fruits in the land: wheat, barley, grapes, figs, pomegranates, olives and dates (translated honey in the King James Version, Deut. 8:8). The law of first fruits required the farmer to mark the first ripened grain in the field or fruit on the trees, and present them in Jerusalem. This food was not burnt on the altar as a sacrifice, but was used to provide food for the many priests at the Temple.

The moment the farmer observed his first ripened fruit, he marked it with a string and declared it *bikurim*, or the first fruits, which were harvested after the fruit completely ripened. Rabbis taught that a farmer should offer one-sixteenth of his produce for the first fruits. After the ripening of the fruits, the farmer would take a basket and place the barley at the bottom, then the wheat, olives (or oil), dates, pomegranates, and figs. Others brought seven different baskets holding one of each of the seven foods. The poor farmer used a simple wicker basket, and the rich often brought gold or silver-plated baskets.

THE TWENTY-FOUR DISTRICTS

The land of Israel from Dan to Beersheba was divided among the tribes. Pre-arranged tribal land grants were secured by the twelve tribes, Joseph being two: Ephraim and Manasseh. The thirteenth tribe was Levi, whose sons were the thousands of priests at the Temple. The

Levites were given no land inheritance, as their personal inheritance was to minister to the Lord daily at the sacred House in Jerusalem (Deut. 10:9).

Few Believers realize that Israel and Jerusalem were both divided into twenty–four districts, or divisions. Each district took turns appearing at the Temple, and these districts were represented by God-fearing Jews who came to the House of the Lord twice a year. The worshippers slept overnight in the central town square, and were awakened in the morning by the officer in charge who would shout out the verse, "Arise! Let us go up to Zion, to the Lord our God" (Jer. 31:6).

As the worshippers approached Jerusalem, leading the group was a man playing a reed flute, and behind him was a sacrificial ox whose horns were covered with gold. There was an olive wreath crown on its head that bore the seven fruits of the land in a basket. The large procession was welcomed by the city officials. After arriving at the Temple, the Levite choir began singing the thirtieth Psalms accompanied by musical instruments. When the rituals and worship were concluded, the men of the districts bowed after leaving their baskets at the southwest corner of the altar, where they were distributed among the twenty-four courses of priests.

There were twenty-four districts in Israel, and twenty-four divisions in Jerusalem for the twenty-four courses of priests who ministered at the Temple. At the time of Moses, the ordinary priests were divided into eight weekly divisions: four from Eleazar's descendants and four from Ithamar's. At the time of David and of Solomon's Temple, the priests were organized into twenty-four divisions—sixteen from Eleazar's descendants and eight from Ithamar's. Each week, a different division of priests were in charge of the service for seven days (1 Chron. 9:25), with the service beginning on a Sabbath and concluding on the following Sabbath. Afterward, they exchanged with a new course, except during the three main festivals when all twenty-four courses were working (1 Chron. 24:7-18). In a census recorded in 1 Chronicles 23:2-6, there were 38,000 Levites from age thirty and beyond. Of these, 24,000 were appointed to oversee the work of the Lord.

The twenty-four courses are significant in the Apocalypse of John, as before the throne of God in the Heavenly Temple there are twenty-four elders sitting on twenty-four thrones, with harps and golden vials full of a sweet fragrance which is the prayers of the saints. These twenty-four are seen in chapter 4 with gold crowns on their heads, falling down in worship. In chapter 5 they are singing a new song and worshiping the Lamb; and also in Revelation 7:1, 11:16, 14:3 and 19:4. Throughout the entire vision of John, these twenty-four elders never leave the Heavenly Temple and remain before the throne of God in worship.

These are representative of the twenty-four courses of priests who minister the entire year at the Temple in Jerusalem—one course for an entire week. These elders remain in one location during the entire seven years of tribulation. This heavenly pattern was also seen in the earthly Temple as, according to Jewish tradition, half of the twenty-four courses in the priesthood were divided and lived permanently in Jerusalem. The others were scattered as far as Jericho. Thus, there was a remnant of priests that remained in the Holy City, just as these twenty-four elders dwell continually in the presence of God.

Later, there are 144,000 Jewish men (12 times 12,000), with twelve thousand from each tribe, who are on the heavenly Mount Zion with harps, singing and worshipping the Lamb. These are the first fruits among the Jews to receive the Messiah during the tribulation and are caught up from the earthly to the heavenly Jerusalem during the mid-point of the tribulation (Rev. 14).

The heavenly twenty-four elders are possibly the twelve sons of Jacob from the Old Covenant and the twelve apostles of Christ from the New Covenant. The Old Covenant prophets revealed numerous end-time judgments of God coming to the earth, and the New Testament reveals the wrath of the Lamb that will strike the nations.

Heavenly worship is continuous during the seven years of tribulation, and harps are mentioned three times. The first harp players are the twenty-four elders who sing prior to the Lamb (Christ) opening the seven-sealed book. Their song is an appreciation to Christ for redeeming people and making them kings and priests (or a kingdom of priests, Rev. 5:10), to rule and reign on earth. This is the imagery of the Feast of Trumpets, also known as the coronation of the king, where the church is before the throne where the beasts, elders, angels, and ten thousand times ten thousand and thousands of thousands begin to worship (Rev. 5:8-11).

The second harp scene is where the 144,000 Jews appear in heaven singing a new song that no other men can sing, playing harps and being identified as the "first fruits unto the Lamb," as they have no moral or spiritual defilement and are redeemed from among men (Rev. 14:1-4). These words used in this section of Revelation are clear allusions to Passover (being redeemed), Unleavened Bread (no defilement), and First Fruits—all three spring feasts.

The third harp players appear in chapter 15, where a multitude stands on the sea of glass that appears like fire and announces they overcame the antichrist (beast), his mark, and his name (Rev. 15:2). These harp players are a group of overcomers who sing the song of Moses, which is the song that was sung after Pharaoh and his armies drowned in the sea (see Exodus 15). These singers introduce the last seven plagues to be released upon the earth by seven angels (see Rev. 15). This imagery is a picture of the judgment process on the Day of Atonement, as God prepares to release judgment on men who would no longer repent of their evil deeds (Rev. 9:20; 16:9; 16:11).

Just as these three harps are symbolically linked to the feasts of Israel, the blowing of the daily trumpets of the priests also carry a prophetic connotation with them. Each day the priests would blast their silver trumpets, blowing seven times, three different blasts. According to tradition, the first blast was to proclaim God's kingdom, the second God's Divine Providence in the affairs of Israel, and the third the final judgment. Three were blown when the gates of the Temple were unlocked and opened, and following the drink offering as it was poured out. The third was poured as the Levites prepared to sing and the people worshipped. These three blasts sounded seven times, and they bear an interesting parallel in the book of Revelation.

In the Apocalypse we find a seven-sealed book, seven trumpet judgments, and seven bowl judgments that are poured out on the earth.

On the Sabbath day, a portion of the Song of Moses was sung; and in Revelation, those who gain victory over the beast appear in heaven, and the song of Moses is sung as those coming out of tribulation now enter their Sabbath of rest in heaven.

When attacking Jericho, seven priests with seven ram's horns marched around the city for six days, blowing the horns. On the seventh day, they blew seven times and the walls of the city fell. There are seven heavenly messengers (called angels) with trumpets that will one day sound, and with each blast a new plague will be introduced. However, when the seventh angel sounds the seventh trumpet, the kingdoms of this world will fail and fall, becoming the kingdoms of God (Rev. 10:7; 11:15), just as Jericho fell into Israel's hands on the seventh day with the seven shofar blasts. When the seventh angel pours out his vial upon the earth in Revelation 16:17, the city of Babylon will divide into three sections and eventually be no more, in what I call the Jericho effect.

God's original intent was for the nation of Israel to be a kingdom of priests, in which every person was a priest and minister to God (Exod. 19:5, 6). The sins of the tribes in the wilderness, including murmuring and worshipping a golden calf, caused God to focus on the tribe of Levi, making his sons the true priesthood through Aaron, Moses's brother.

THE REBEL'S BEATING

Since the church is considered a royal priesthood and a holy nation (1 Pet. 2:9), the blessings imparted to the priest and the strict punishments for errant priests can be applicable to the New Testament priesthood of Believers. Several statements made by Christ were understood by his listeners to apply to the punishment given to disobedient priests at the Temple.

During the night shifts, the priests were assigned to keep watch over the gates leading into the Temple compound and the sacred places of the Temple. Remember, there were gold and silver vessels, along with offerings in chambers, and thieves who stole the treasures knew they would become wealthy overnight. A severe punishment was applied to any priest caught sleeping during his watch at night. The captain of the House would publically reprimand him, strip him of his garments, and beat him with rods.

This imagery is concealed in a warning Christ gave the churches in Revelation 16:15, *"Behold, I am coming as a thief. Blessed is he who watches, and keeps his garments, lest he walks naked and they see his shame."* Believers are continually commanded to *watch and pray* (Matt. 24:43; Mark 13:33, 37), which means to set a watch to prevent the enemy from overtaking you, and to stay awake so you will not be found sleeping at Christ's return.

In a parable, Christ spoke of being a wise steward over the Lord's goods and being prepared for His sudden return, where each steward will give an account of their actions to the master. The servant who says the master delays his coming will begin to be drunk and mistreat the servants in the Lord's house. When the master returns, he will severely punish the unwise and proud servant, as it is written, *"And that servant who knew his master's will, and did not prepare himself or do according to his will, shall be beaten with many stripes. But he who did not know, yet committed things deserving of stripes, shall be beaten with few"* (Luke 12:47-48).

This beating would have been understood by the Jews as a rebel's beating for the unfaithful servant. Among the Jews, there were two possible systems of scourging: forty stripes minus one, which Christ received at the hands of the Romans, and the rebel's beating. The former was conducted after a trial, and the latter needed no trial. Before Christ's crucifixion, He was scourged with a Roman whip, and also beaten with the palms of His accusers' hands. This beating with the hands was a form of a rebel's beating (John 19:3) in the Roman period.

These rebel's beatings could be done with the hands, fists, a rod or a whip. For example, when a priest defiled the law, a beating was inflicted upon him without a trial. This is one reason that Paul was physically beaten by the Jews three times with rods, as he was considered a traitor and a rebel against the Jewish customs (Acts 18:13; 2 Cor. 11:25). Stephen was stoned by a group of Jews, because it was considered within bounds to stone any heretic who opposed the laws and traditions. Thus Stephen was viewed by his enemies as a rebel against God (Acts 7:54-59). At Stephen's death, a chief rabbi named Saul of Tarsus was consenting to the death of this rebel named Stephen.

On one occasion, Christ was entering the Temple compound when He saw the devious money changers who had turned the Temple sacrifices into a profitable business, and were ignoring the true purpose of God's House being a place of prayer and intimacy to the Father. Jesus grabbed a whip and began his own "rebel's beating" (John 2:14-16). Perhaps He was recalling the Proverb that "a wound cleanses away evil and stripes the inward part of the belly" (Prov. 20:30), or perhaps Psalm 89:31-32, "If they break my statutes and do not keep my commandments, then I will punish their transgression with the rod, and their iniquity with stripes."

The reason for sharing this is that certain parables related to the coming of Christ clearly reveal that, at His return, there will be a division between the wise and foolish virgins, the faithful and unfaithful servants, and the good and bad servants. The wise, faithful and good are blessed and rewarded, whereas the foolish, unfaithful and bad are punished and are not permitted to enter the wedding (see Matthew 25). According to Christ, two are in the field, grinding at the meal or in bed, and one is taken and the other is left. The faithful in Christ are taken and the unfaithful or unbelieving will remain on earth at His return.

It is important to understand that there are people who have knowledge of Christ, but not an intimate covenant relationship. These will not be prepared to meet Christ, so they must go through the tribulation. These individuals will have enough knowledge of events to know that they must be willing to be beheaded for their testimony (Rev. 6:9; 20:4). These are part of the great multitude that comes out of great tribulation and are seen in heaven after making their robes white in the blood of the Lamb" (Rev. 7:14).

Three groups are identified in Revelation. The overcoming church is the multitude seen in chapter 5, singing praises to the Lamb with the angels, beasts and elders. These Believers are rewarded at the bema

(Rev. 11:18) and assigned as kings, priest, and rulers on the earth during the thousand-year kingdom of Christ on earth. Those living during the tribulation and who make their robes white will service God before His throne in His Temple day and night (Rev. 7:14). The third group is the 144,000 Jewish converts who were redeemed from the earth, and who will follow the Lamb wherever He goes (Rev. 14:4). Those beheaded by the antichrist will be resurrected and will rule and live with Christ for a thousand years (Rev. 20:4).

When I hear discussions about how the church must go through the future tribulation and suffer at the hands of the antichrist, I am reminded of the *law of separation* found throughout the Scripture and the Laws of God demanding a separation between the holy and unholy, clean and unclean, sacred and profane (see Lev. 21). The parables explicitly point out this law of separation. The sheep are separated from the goats (Matt. 25:33); the good fish from the bad fish (Matt. 13:47-48); and the wheat (children of the kingdom) from the tares (children of the world, Matt. 13:30). Among the ten virgins, the five wise entered the marriage and the five foolish were shut out (Matt. 25). Christ also separates the profitable or faithful servants from the unprofitable ones (Matt. 25:30).

When Christ returns to earth, there is a judgment in the Valley of Jehoshaphat in Jerusalem for those still alive after the tribulation. Those with the mark of the beast are separated from those without the mark, as sheep and goats, and wheat and tare are separated in a field (Joel 3:2; Matt. 25:32-46). The law of separation began with God separating Cain, the first murderer, marking his forehead, and sending him as a vagabond into the land of wandering, away from the presence of the Lord (Gen. 4:1-16). The final separation will be at the Great White Throne Judgment, when those whose names were not inscribed in the book of life are forever separated from the righteous (Rev. 20:11-15). Only when the righteous become unrighteous will judgments come upon them, along with the unrighteous (Jer. 44:8-14).

Before the future tribulation begins, the totally righteous (the church without spot, wrinkle or blemish) must be separated from the totally unrighteous and the unfaithful or rebellious servants (note the parables). Then the tribulation will release the season of God's vengeance (Nahum 1:2) and wrath (Rev. 6:16; 16:1). The prophet Nahum said that God reserves His wrath for his enemies (Nah. 1:2), and Isaiah wrote that God sends His wrath to destroy the sinner off the earth (Isa. 13:9).

The New Testament says that the wrath of God abides on those who do not believe in the Son (John 3:36), and the wrath of God is revealed from heaven against all ungodliness (Rom. 1:18). Paul also wrote that wrath and indignation are upon those that obey not the truth, including tribulation and anguish (Rom. 2:8). Not one passage in the Bible places the wrath of God upon a truly righteous person walking in holiness and purity of the Word and the Spirit.

God's wrath is not for the righteous, as the righteous have been set free from the wrath of God, and there is no willful impurity for God to judge. If we are justified (placed in right standing) by Christ's blood, we shall be saved from wrath (Rom. 5:9). Paul said that Christ has delivered us from the wrath to come (1 Thess. 1:10). He also said, "God did not appoint us to wrath, but to obtain salvation through our Lord Jesus Christ, who died for us, that whether we wake or sleep, we should live together with Him. Therefore comfort each other and edify one another, just as you also are doing" (1 Thess. 5:9-11). Jesus spoke of those who are "accounted worthy to obtain the (age to come)..." (Luke 20:35). Luke also recorded Christ's words:

> *"But take heed to yourselves, lest your hearts be weighed down with carousing, drunkenness, and cares of this life, and that Day come on you unexpectedly. For it will come as a snare on all those who dwell on the face of the whole earth. Watch therefore, and pray always that you may be counted worthy to escape all these things that will come to pass, and to stand before the Son of Man."*
>
> – LUKE 21:34-36 (NKJV)

As Believers set a priestly watch over their souls, they are also required to pray to be found worthy to escape the wrath coming to the earth. The Greek idea of being deemed *worthy* is to weigh something on a scale to see its exact worth or value, hence the idea of counting something. The worth is discovered in the weighing process. We can look into the Scriptures and see if our private life aligns with our public testimony, and we can judge ourselves based upon our obedience to the Word. When God wrote with His finger on the palace wall in Babylon, he informed King Belshazzar that he had been weighed in the balance and found wanting (Dan. 5:27). This Babylonian king was drinking from the sacred Temple vessels and had fallen short of obeying the true God. That night he was judged unworthy of Divine protection and his kingdom fell into the armies of the Medes and Persians (See Dan. 5).

In one of Christ's wedding parables, the king was preparing for his son's wedding and those within the kingdom were called to attend. However, the king's servants were too busy making money, selling and farming, and they made light of the invitation and ignored the king's decree. Then the king said to his servants, "The wedding is ready, but those who were invited were not worthy. Therefore go into the highways, and as many as you find, invite to the wedding" (Matt. 22:8-9). The question is will you be found worthy when the great shofar sounds at Christ's return, or will you be found idle, bogged down with cares, and in unbelief?

Paul summed up my thoughts when he wrote:

> *"We are bound to thank God always for you, brethren, as it is fitting, because your faith grows exceedingly, and the love of every one of you all abounds toward each other, so that we ourselves boast of you among the churches of God for your patience and faith in all your persecutions and tribulations that you endure, which is manifest evidence of the righteous judgment of God, that you may be counted worthy of the kingdom of God, for which you also suffer; since it is a righteous thing with God to repay with tribulation those who trouble you."*
>
> – 2 Thess. 1:3-7 (NKJV)

FIRST FRUITS AND THE FIRSTBORN

It is a powerful revelation to discover how all nations are blessed through Israel, a small piece of real estate with a legacy linked to a Hebrew named Abraham. The nation of Israel had no actual name until Jacob had twelve sons who were called the sons of Jacob (Gen 34:7, 13,

25, 27) and the children of Jacob (2 Kings 17:34; 1 Chron. 16:13; Psa. 105:6). When Jacob wrestled the angel, his name was changed from Jacob to Israel, a name whose general meaning is "a prince with God" or "prevailing with God." From that moment of Jacob's wrestling, this tribal family name became the "children of Israel" (Gen. 32:32; 45:21; 46:8; 50:25).

Israel is identified by God Himself with two unique names. God called Israel His son and demanded that Pharaoh "let my son go, that he may serve me" (Exod. 4:23). In this same passage, God added another aspect of His relationship with Israel, when He called them, "My firstborn." The concept of Israel being God's firstborn is unique for several reasons.

First, the founders of Israel were Abraham, Isaac and Jacob. Their wives—Sarah, Rebekah, and Rachel—were barren and unable to conceive children. All three women eventually gave birth: Sarah gave birth to Isaac; Rachel gave birth to Jacob and Esau; and Rebekah gave birth to Joseph and Benjamin.

To birth a nation from three barren wombs of three women makes Israel's conception a supernatural miracle in itself. God demonstrated His presence in the earthly realm through supernatural signs and wonders, often using the natural elements and cosmic activity to prove His power and existence to mankind. However, God desired a family, and this process required a spiritually alert and sensitive man to initiate a special covenant. Abraham was that man to whom God promised a future nation. God Himself predicted that Abraham would be the father of many nations (Gen. 17:5). How does one man's seed form one nation called Israel, yet many nations are promised to Abraham?

The key is that God spoke of Israel as His firstborn son. In Deuteronomy 21, Moses penned a series of laws and instructions concerning the firstborn sons. He stated that the firstborn son is the beginning of a man's strength. The Gentile nations were set in motion after Noah's flood with his sons Shem, Ham and Japheth, who settled in three regions of the earth and whose descendants formed the major ethnic groups of early history. All spoke one language until the Tower of Babel, when the people were dispersed and their languages confused. Each ethnic group clung to their own dialect and people group, thus forming the various nations of the Gentiles. God required a people set apart, a people who would obey His laws and remain pure to bring forth the promised Messiah who would redeem the world.

Israel is the only nation, according to Scripture, that God Himself ordained and birthed from barren wombs to be a holy nation and a chosen people. In the law of the firstborn, the firstborn son received a double blessing, a double portion of goods after the father's death, and the special spoken blessing passed from the father to the firstborn near the time of the father's departure (note Gen. 25:32-34 and Gen. 27:30-36; Deut. 21:17). We see this practice when Jacob is dying and he blesses the two sons of Joseph, Ephraim and Manasseh, and places them in the tribal clan with his natural birth sons. We see this when the aged patriarch leaned on his staff and spoke the prophetic blessings over the original sons born out of his loins (Gen. 48 and 49).

As God's firstborn, Israel was ordained for a blessing and a birthright. Abraham was given a "stars of heaven and sand of the earth" prophecy (Gen. 22:17). The sand promise represents the natural Jews (Gen. 32:12), and the stars promise is the imagery of a spiritual seed, the church, that makes up the believers of the New Covenant through Christ. The promises for natural Israel are earthly, while the promises for the church are spiritual and heavenly. Paul wrote:

> *"Christ has redeemed us from the curse of the law, having become a curse for us (for it is written, "Cursed is everyone who hangs on a tree"), that the blessing of Abraham might come upon the Gentiles in Christ Jesus..."*
>
> – Gal. 3:13-14 (NKJV)

Israel has a birthright in the earth through Abraham's covenant. In God's law of the firstborn, all males born were originally marked to be priests to God:

> *"...because all the firstborn are Mine. On the day that I struck all the firstborn in the land of Egypt, I sanctified to Myself all the firstborn in Israel, both man and beast. They shall be Mine: I am the LORD."*
>
> – Num. 3:13 (NKJV)

The original intent was that Israel would be a nation of priests and a holy nation of believers who could approach God in sacrifices and worship. The sin of idolatry caused the Almighty to set a mark upon the Levites, granting them special rights and privileges to approach His sacred edifices with sacrifices and offerings. Centuries later, through the New Covenant, all believers who receive Christ have their names inscribed in the heavenly book of life and are part of a new nation and a royal priesthood.

MISTREATING THE FIRSTBORN

Pharaoh, king of Egypt, was clearly warned that if he refused to allow God's firstborn son Israel to freely depart from Israel, (God knew he would resist), then the firstborn son of Pharaoh and the rest of the Egyptians would be slain (Exod. 4:23). The tenth plague in Egypt was initiated with the angel of death who passed over each Israelite home that was marked with the lamb's blood, but entered the unprotected doors of the Egyptians, striking the darts of death into the hearts of the firstborn sons, firstborn slaves, and firstborn animals of the Egyptians (Exod. 11:5).

Throughout history, entire empires have made attempts to attack and even destroy God's firstborn nation, ignoring a warning that said God would bless those that bless Israel and curse those that curse Israel (Gen. 12:3). The Jewish historian Josephus narrates that, when the Egyptians pursued the Hebrews to the Red Sea, six hundred chariots, fifty thousand horsemen, and two hundred thousand footmen were behind the Israelites as the Red Sea was before them. God made a passage through the sea and, when the Egyptian army entered the same path, they were killed when the waters closed upon them.

When the Assyrians advanced toward Jerusalem and encircled the walls with intent to invade, God sent an angel to slay 185,000 soldiers. When Belshazzar, king of Babylon, brought the seized vessels from the Temple to drink from at his all-night party, God became a party crasher by using the Medes and Persians to overthrow the Babylonians in one night!

In AD 70, the tenth legion of Rome seemingly got away with

seizing the Temple treasures, burning the Temple in Jerusalem, sacking the city, and taking the surviving Jews away in chains. However, the Western Roman Empire eventually collapsed and was overrun by Germanic tribes.

Centuries ago, it was said that the sun never sets on the British Empire. Britain had colonized much of Africa and the Middle East. However, when the holocaust ended, a ship of survivors headed to the port in Haifa, with no home or homeland, desiring to settle in British-controlled Palestine. They were turned away by the British. The cold hearted and calloused political maneuver backfired, and eventually Britain gave up Palestine into the control of the Jews and Arabs.

It should be clear from historical narratives that God defends Israel because God defends His covenants. Since Israel is God's firstborn, those who mistreat the firstborn will suffer consequences, while those who bless the firstborn will receive favor from the Almighty.

Because of the lack of prophetic teaching in America, people in the United States are often ignorant of the fact that Israel has a covenant with God. They have a covenant for the land of Israel and for the city of Jerusalem, and the entire territory is marked and set aside by the Lord Himself as the nation where the future kingdom of the Messiah will be set up for a thousand years! When Christians work against Israel, they are working against God's covenant. When anyone, including individuals, nations or empires, touches Israel, God said:

> *"For thus says the LORD of hosts: "He sent Me after glory, to the nations which plunder you; for he who touches you touches the apple of His eye. For surely I will shake My hand against them, and they shall become spoil for their servants."*

> – ZECH. 2:8-9 (NJKV)

The apple of the eye is a Hebrew idiom that refers to the dark part of the eye where the pupil is located. The idea is that, when you look at someone else's eyes up close, you can actually see a reflection of your-self in their pupil. In Hebrew this reflection is called "the little man of the eye." Israel being the apple of God's eye indicates to me that, when God sees Israel with His eyes, He sees a reflection of Himself.

Israel is His firstborn son, and they carried God's laws, Word, and hopes of the Messianic kingdom throughout their history. In the passage in Zechariah, the word toucheth in Hebrew can mean to "lay a hand upon in the form of violently striking or trying to destroy." The idea conveys that anyone who would attempt to do harm to Israel would be poking God in the pupil of His eye. In turn, God would initiate retaliation against the culprits and shake His hand against them. This phrase refers to God shaking the people or the nations to bring about their eventual destruction.

No other nation in the Bible, except Israel, has been given a direct promise from God to endure as long as the sun and moon exist (Ps. 89:2-3; 35-37). Jerusalem (called Salem in Gen. 14:18), the Holy City and capital of Israel, has been besieged twenty-three times, attacked about fifty-two times, and totally destroyed twice. The nation of Israel has been ruled by Gentile powers or empires seven times since the 4th century BC. They were ruled by the Romans, Byzantines, Muslims, Crusaders, Mamelukes, Ottoman Turks, and British. Finally, in 1948, Israel once again became a nation under the control of the Jewish people.

Here is the miracle. Jerusalem has been rebuilt, and today the nation is a tourist's mecca that draws millions of pilgrims from every nation. Israel is the size of the state of Rhode Island, but they have the fourth best military, and they lead among the world's nations in medical, military, and other forms of technology. Yet they have existed as a rebirthed nation only since 1948! If a person does not believe in God, they have never studied the miracle of the Jews, Jerusalem, and Israel.

CHAPTER 11

THE BITTERNESS OF CHESVAN— SURVIVING WINTER

THE JEWISH CALENDAR consists of twelve months with an additional month (Adar II) added every four years to ensure that the feasts fall on the proper months. Israel's last of the seven appointed festivals, Tabernacles, concludes in the seventh month on the 21st day. From that moment there are about six months until the spring, which repeats the festival cycle beginning with Passover. The eighth month on the Jewish calendar cycle is Chesvan, one of only two months that contains no festival, called fast, or special events. The other month is Elul; however, Elul is the month of preparation for Feast of Trumpets and the Days of Awe that climax on the Day of Atonement.

Chesvan is the month when winter begins. At times it is called the "naked month," as the fields have been harvested, the fruit has been plucked from the tree, rotting leaves are on the ground, and nearly all of creation appears naked. Even certain animals go into hibernation and the growth of most living plants slows.

We see this in the west as well. During our winter months, the days are shorter and the nights are longer. Many weeks the sun is veiled behind a sheet of lowering grey clouds. The sound of the birds is silenced and the trees of the forest appear as an army of naked skeletons, frozen in time with their arms raised in surrender. In a few places on earth, the days are dark, and this darkness continues throughout the winter. Sometimes people sit in rooms lit with artificial sunlight to combat the depression that can follow when there is no light.

Chesvan as the first month of winter paints several applications. The flow of human life follows a circle of life similar to the four seasons in a year. We begin in spring, move into summer, and eventually reach fall in which we receive the harvest of our life's labors. As we approach winter, we reach our time of retirement, grandchildren, and reflection on life. We can feel the atmosphere shift from the warm early fall to the chill of late fall, and then the cold wind of winter.

I remember when my dad approached the last days of winter. In the final twelve months, his quality of life was interrupted by a weary mind and a physical body that refused to cooperate with his desire to remain active. Diabetes had taken its toll and he would sit in a chair most of the day. The end of winter was coming—the final day of his life on earth. But the cycle did not end, because his next moment in time would find him in a new world with perfect health!

When Paul was jailed in Rome, he penned his last epistle to Timothy, his spiritual son. Paul knew his departure was at hand, and that he would soon be offered as a martyr for Christ (2 Tim 4:6). However, at the conclusion of his letter, Paul asked to personally see several people face-to-face before his death.

Paul requested that they make diligence in coming to him and to "come before winter" (2 Time 4:1). Paul was in Rome and the journey was made by ship. Winter storms on the Mediterranean were dangerous and could be deadly (see Acts 27). The roads and mountains can be blanketed with snow or ice, and transportation might be difficult. This has both a natural and a spiritual application. Naturally, he knew the season of transition meant that easy travel would become difficult and dangerous. He was aware that winter had arrived for him and his ministry. The spring of newness, the summer of planning and traveling, and the fall of harvesting souls was now passed. He was in chains, in prison, and awaiting death by beheading. Nero had set Rome on fire and blamed the Christians, with Paul being the alleged leader of this nonexistent uprising.

Paul was known throughout Asia among thousands of his converts, and numerous churches were started during his missionary journeys. However, the false rumor that filtered from Rome of Paul's arrest for initiating the fire at Circus Maximus, the Roman shops, and the market place apparently was believed by some in the church. Paul wrote, "This thou know, that all they which are in Asia be turned away from me..." (2 Tim 1:15). Ministry partners had broken fellowship and converts were accepting a false allegation. Winter had come and instead of being held in the warm arms of compassionate followers of Christ, Paul was begging for his closest friends to come and say farewell—before winter.

THE WORLD WILL HAVE ITS WINTER

The world has experienced many seasons since the fall of Adam. However, the future time of tribulation will be the longest season of winter in global history. When Christ warned His disciples of the future trouble surrounding Jerusalem and Judea, He said:

> *"And pray that your flight may not be in winter or on the Sabbath. For then there will be great tribulation, such as has not been since the beginning of the world until this time, no, nor ever shall be."*
>
> – MATT. 24:20-21 (NKJV)

The flight referred to is the sudden departure of the Jewish people from Jerusalem and the surrounding region, when the armies of the enemy are preparing to surround the walls and lay siege to the city. The modern city of Jerusalem has tens of thousands of Orthodox and ultra-Orthodox Jews who honor the Sabbath and, by Jewish law, are limited to the length they can journey on the Sabbath. If these people were required to get out of the city on the Sabbath, many would never go beyond the distances permitted to travel on the Sabbath. They would be stuck in the city when the enemy invaded. The winter referred to here is literal. Jerusalem is 2,500 feet in elevation, and from December to February it can be cold and they might even see an accumulation of snow. It would be very difficult if the Jews were forced to flee Jerusalem in the heart of winter.

The future of the world is a winter without God. This winter season is seven years of tribulation, with the final forty-two months being the greater tribulation (Rev. 11:2; 12:14). For the majority of the Gentile nations, the heavens will be as brass, as spiritual blessings will cease and bowls of wrath will be poured out upon the nations. Just as every man's winter is the time of his departure from this life to the next, the tribulation is the world's winter that will initiate the pale horse and rider called death and hell, whose hooves will beat a path from nation to nation, city to city, door to door, and fire arrows of death into the hearts of the population. The unbelievers are headed to the darkest winter known to mankind (Dan. 12:1).

Now back to the Believers. Winter is not only a season when the natural world seems asleep, and not only a representation of the finality of life and the season when circumstances are bleak and life is dull; but winter is also when it seems that God is doing nothing. All of life seems to stop and become dormant. We have passed our spring season, our great redemption through the Lamb of God at Passover, and our sanctification by removing the leaven at Unleavened Bread. We have experienced Pentecost and the infilling of the Spirit, and the Days of Awe and Seasons of Joy through the fall feasts.

Yet, winter comes and we know it is before us. You can curse it, accept it, be chilled by it, or be thrilled with it. Here is why. During Israel's winters, it rains. Without the winter rains there would be no spring flowers. Without winter, the hard ground would not be softened to receive the seeds that will give birth to new life and harvest. Without rain, the cisterns would be dry and famine would result. God, in His cycles of seasons in life, has a reason why, even throughout the normal year, we hit days or weeks of winter.

Winter is when you have supported God's work through tithes and offerings, and suddenly you are handed a pink slip at work. Winter is an accident that disables a loved one for life and changes your routine from being care free to being a care giver. Winter expresses itself during economic downturns, or when addictions strike, or when depression dulls a once happy soul.

JESUS WAS REJOICING IN WINTER

The Gospel of John reveals what Christ was doing during winter: "Now it was the Feast of Dedication in Jerusalem, and it was winter" (John 10:22-23). The English translation uses the word dedication, but we know this celebration as Hanukkah, also named the festival of lights. It was a custom for all males to attend the three main Torah feasts yearly. However, Hanukkah was not a Torah festival, but an inter-testament celebration, as the events leading to this important Jewish season occurred between the final Old Testament prophet Malachi and the appearing of Christ. Hanukkah often falls in the month of December, which can be chilly in the evenings in Jerusalem. In winter, Jesus attended the Feast of Dedication, recalling over 198 years prior the defeat of the wicked Antiochus and the cleansing of the Temple.

While celebrating the victory, Christ was challenged to reveal if He was the Christ. When Christ revealed the truth of His identity, the religious Jews took up rocks to stone Him because He called himself God (John 10:33). This was in winter. Christ entered Jerusalem with the intent of rejoicing and celebrating the memorial of the miracle of Hanukkah; yet religious resisters to His ministry were intent on hindering Him.

Christ being in Jerusalem in winter is an example for us to follow when we approach our own winters. Chesvan is the beginning of winter and a sign of an empty, void, dull and rather lifeless season. However, among the Jews, in the ninth month a special Festival is set—right in the heart of winter. This simple fact is a reflection of an important truth for you and me. In the midst of our winter seasons throughout the year, during difficult circumstances, or when the winter path is leading to the end of our earthly walk, God will prepare a season of refreshing and celebration—in the midst of winter.

The winter season is a normal process and part of the natural cycle of life. When we humans move from late fall to early winter, knowing our earthly clock is ticking down to zero, it may seem overwhelming and depressing. For several years I observed my own father, Fred Stone, enter his season of winter. He was always a very active and energetic man, continually fasting, praying daily, and living to preach. With diabetes and dialysis, his body became very thin, his eyes grew dim, and his strength diminished. He was barely surviving in the heart of the winter season.

One night I was driving him home from our office. In my mind, I could hear the clock ticking, moving forward toward eternity one second at a time. Every moment with him was a precious memory being made. As I pulled into the driveway, I took a deep breath and prepared to ask him a question.

I asked, "Dad, you won't be here much longer. What goes through your mind when you think about passing on?" Silence followed. He turned and with a slight grin said, "Oh I'm not worried about dying. In fact, I believe when that time comes it will be a glorious experience to pass from here to heaven."

Then I realized that winter is not the death of all things. Just as when December 31st arrives, it is the last day of an old year and one second after midnight the beginning of a new year, so it is with winter. It is the end of one era and the beginning of another; the end of one age and the initiation of a new one; and the end of the earthly to enter the heavenly. It is difficult for a true believer to be sad about winter and their departure, when the best is yet to come!

CHAPTER 12

THE MYSTERY OF
THE SHOFAR

IN THE MONTH of Elul, the shofar is sounded each day. The rabbis teach that the Hebrew letters in the word "ELUL" form an acronym for the phrase, "I am for my Beloved and my Beloved is for me." The idea of blowing the shofar each day on Elul is linked to the second return of Moses to Mount Sinai. It was on Pentecost that Moses received the Ten Commandments. However, when he saw the golden calf, Moses broke the stone tablets on the ground. After judging the rebels, grinding up the golden calf, and arranging the tribes, Moses went up again on the mount on the 1st of Elul, where he remained for forty days. He returned on the Day of Atonement with a new set of commandments on stone.

A shofar was blown on each of the twenty-nine days of Elul to remind the people not to sin while Moses was out of their sight, face to face with God. Today the shofar is blown during the twenty-nine days as a reminder for the people to inspect their own souls and actions in preparation for the great Day of Atonement.

The word trumpet, when read in the English Bible, paints the image of a brass or silver trumpet blown in an orchestra. In the Scripture, the trumpet can be a silver trumpet or the horn of a kosher animal, called a shofar. The idea of using a shofar, normally a ram's horn, stems from the event in Genesis 22 where shortly after Abraham laid Isaac on the altar, a ram was caught in the thicket and became the replacement sacrifice for Isaac. The Jewish tradition says that Abraham removed both horns from the ram, and the horns were preserved by the Jewish people through Isaac and Jacob, and were even carried to Egypt. Later, when Moses blew the shofar, the tradition states it was one of the horns of the ram of Abraham.

After departing from Egypt, the Israelites came to Mount Sinai where God came down on the mountain in a cloud and His voice was the sound of a mighty shofar (Exod. 19:16; 20:18). Thus, the blast of a shofar became equated with the actual voice of God.

PREPARING A SHOFAR

Years ago I attended a Hebraic conference in Florida where a Jewish man demonstrated the way to prepare a shofar. Once the horn is removed from the animal, the inside must be thoroughly cleaned from the dead flesh. If the dried flesh remains, when the shofar is blown, a terrible odor is released from the horn. This man had hot sand in a wooden box, and he demonstrated how a person would lay the shofar in the hot sand and twist the horn to form more detailed curves. The third process was to bore a hole at the top of the shofar to provide a place for the air to enter from the person blowing into it. The final process was to polish the outside of the horn, as natural horns are actually weather worn and quite dull in appearance until they are polished.

While sitting in the class, I was quickened to the interesting parallels between the shofar and the spiritual body, which is the temple of the Holy Spirit (1 Cor. 3:15-16). First, the shofar must be removed from the animal, just as you must separate yourself from the world when you come to Christ. The first challenge, once you have been separated, is to deal with the desires of your flesh and remove those sins that could easily weigh you down in the race. The third process is to prepare an opening in your spirit so the wind of the Holy Spirit can blow and move through you. The polishing effect is when God places you on public display after preparing you for His work and ministry.

That day, I became aware that each human body has its own built-in shofar. When you open your mouth to inhale and exhale, your mouth becomes the "mouth" of the shofar and emits sounds. The wind pipe, or esophagus, becomes the stem of the shofar. The wind pipe connects to the belly, and Christ taught that from our belly (innermost being) would flow rivers of living water (John 7:38). The sound of praise emits from our innermost being and exits from the opening in our mouth. When God created man, He placed within each human a built-in shofar.

I once heard a great musician explain the different categories of musical instruments. All musical instruments are divided into four classifications: wind, brass, percussion, and stringed instruments. The strings include guitars, pianos, violins, harps and any instrument in which strings creates the sound. Brass instruments include the horn, trombone, tuba, and brass saxophone. The flute, the bassoon, piccolo, reed, and clarinet are wind instruments, while percussion instruments are drums, cymbals, and the tambourine.

Scriptures such as Ezekiel 28 and Isaiah 14, which most scholars believe refer to Satan, indicate that he was an anointed cherub who was created with timbrels and pipes—words that are used to describe musical instruments (Ezek. 28:13; Isa. 14:11). However, Satan was never created with the trumpet, as the sound of the trumpet (shofar) was strictly reserved for God Himself. The Lord ensured that mankind's future archenemy would be missing the loud blast of the trumpet.

However, God created a built-in trumpet within all human beings, as man was created in the image of God and would replace the praise and worship missing from heaven after the fall of Satan and his angels.

The fall festival of Rosh Hashanah is also called Yom Teruah, or "the day of the blowing of the shofar." This was the theme God established for this day, the Feast of Trumpets (Num. 29:1). In ancient times the shofar was blown for Holy Days and new moons, as well as over the burnt offerings and sacrifices (Num. 10:10). The joyful sound of silver trumpets announced the Jubilee, called in Hebrew the *yovel*, a word meaning, "the blast of the horn" (Lev. 25:9). The shofar was blasted prior to a war and following a victory in battle.

Kings were also crowned with the blowing of trumpets and shofars. The Festival of Trumpets is also known as the coronation of the king and the Day of Judgment. Among the ancient Jews, the heavenly sign of the seventh month (Tishrei) is Libra, which represents scales and a balance of judgment. This month among ancients was known as a time of reckoning.

In the future are two major times when there will be blasts from the heavenly trumpets, believed to be heavenly shofars, and both are connected with a resurrection and an ingathering. The first will be the trump of God, which will emit a series of sounds when Christ returns to raise the dead in Christ and to gather together the living to meet Him in the air (1 Thess. 4:16-17; Eph. 1:9-10). The sound of God's trump will be a series of blasts in a quick fashion, as the Bible indicates that those living will be changed from a corruptible to an incorruptible body at the "sound of the last trump" (1 Cor. 15:52). Since on the day of the Feast of Trumpets there are over one hundred blasts, the last trump is the last in the series of blasts and is also considered the great blast. This is the final sound made, which is the longest and the loudest.

Omitting the trumpets sounded from the heavenly Temple by the seven angels, there is a second major shofar sound that will be heard throughout the earth. When Christ returns to earth with the saints, He sends angels with the sound of a great trumpet to gather His elect from the four regions of the earth (Matt. 24:31).

THE BIG SHOFAR

According to the Jewish laws of the shofar, there are three levels of the shofar. The best choice is the horn of a ram. The second would be the horn of a kosher animal, and the third a non-kosher animal, if a kosher animal is not available. These three are also identified as the *big* shofar, the *regular* shofar, and the *small* shofar. Awakening that leads to redemption is always a theme associated with the shofar, as the one hundred blasts on the Feast of Trumpets precede the great Day of Atonement in which Israel's redemption or judgment will be sealed.

At the conclusion of the great tribulation, Christ returns with the armies of heaven to intercept the nations gathered against Jerusalem and intervene in the planned destruction of Israel and the Jewish people. When the King of kings arrives in Jerusalem, here is His first assignment:

> *"And He will send His angels with a great sound of a trumpet, and they will gather together His elect from the four winds, from one end of heaven to the other."*
>
> – MATT. 24:31 (NKJV)

At the rapture, there is an ingathering of the dead in Christ and those righteous overcomers who are living at the time of the sound of the last trumpet (1 Cor. 15:52). I believe evidence from a Biblical and Hebraic perspective tends to point more to a pre-tribulation gathering together of the overcomers who have been faithful to Christ. But this ingathering mentioned above is "after the tribulation in those days," (Matt. 24:29). Notice that Christ sends angels (plural) and not one particular angel, to blast the sound of a great trumpet to the north, south, east and west to call forth the elect who have survived the tribulation.

Abraham's seed was to be as the sand and the stars. (Gen. 22:17). Sand is earthly and stars are heavenly, and both were created by God Himself. There is a natural seed of Abraham—the Jews with a Jewish mother—and there is a spiritual seed—those Believers who have received Christ. Natural Jews and true Believers both call Abraham the father of the faith (John 8:39; Rom. 4:1; Gal. 3:9, 14-18).

The two horns on the ram of Abraham were the original shofars. One horn gives the imagery of the first resurrection and the dead in Christ at the rapture, while the spiritual seed of Abraham will be caught up to the heavenly city to rejoice, receive rewards, and be spared God's wrath. At the end of the tribulation, the second horn is the picture of the great trumpet blown when the Messiah returns to save and deliver the natural seed of Abraham that has survived the tribulation.

So we see that the shofar (trumpet) is used at the resurrection of the dead in Christ (1 Cor. 15:52) and the transformation of the living saints at the gathering together (1 Thess. 4:16-17). Then it is used again during the tribulation as seven angels blast seven trumpets (Rev. 8:2). The final time is the sounding of the great trumpet when Christ returns to earth to rule for a thousand years (Matt. 24:31).

CHAPTER 13

SATAN'S COUNTERFEIT FEASTS

T HE SECULAR WORLD marks the end of the year at midnight, December 31, and the beginning of the New Year one second after midnight, beginning January 1. The Jewish yearly cycle has two divisions: the religious and the secular. The religious calendar begins in the early spring on the first month called Nissan, the same month Passover is set. The secular New Year begins on the Feast of Trumpets, which is the first day of the seventh month. Today, the Jewish calendar cycle begins on the Feast of Trumpets or Rosh ha Shanah.

I have always believed and continue to teach that Satan is a master counterfeiter. What he cannot destroy, he attempts to duplicate and corrupt in some manner, thus drawing men away through deception from God's original intent and purpose. God's festivals were set each year and were significant to the entire nation. Over the centuries, the adversary inspired the pagan religions to establish particular days and seasons that became celebrations and ritualistic activities. The particular rituals varied from tribe to tribe and ethnic group to ethnic group, but a closer study will expose certain days of the year as Satan's counterfeit festivals and days.

Just as God appointed key days during the year, followers of the occult, wicca, paganism and such have marked certain days throughout the year. God's seasons bring special favor and blessings, and release forgiveness and prosperity among those in covenant with Him. But these occult seasons do the opposite. They release negative spiritual forces into the atmosphere, and those negative forces can be recognized by Believers whose inner spirits are sharpened to detect the spiritual powers working in the atmosphere.

Just as there are various spiritual blessings released on God's feast days, former occultists reveal that there is an increase in negative spiritual forces (they call it negative energy) released on these dates. Christian intercessors have learned that during these times the following occurs:

- There is an increase in the spiritual movement among demonic forces.

- There is an increase in occult prayers, curses and incantations being offered.

- There is an increase in oppression and depression in the atmosphere.

- These changes in the spiritual atmosphere can be sensed by discerning Believers.

When are these occult seasons, what happens during these cycles, and how can Believers counter the negative atmosphere?

THE OPPOSITES IN TWO KINGDOMS

The first foundational fact is that our enemy is a counterfeiter. He attempts to counterfeit the spiritual blessings of God; yet in reality, he produces an opposite effect:

In God's Kingdom We Find	In Satan's Kingdom is the Opposite
Love	Hate
Joy	Sorrow
Peace	Confusion
Prosperity	Poverty
Mercy	Destruction

Faith	Unbelief
Hope	Hopelessness
Light	Darkness
Life	Death

Please note that Satan is not the opposite of God, as God has no equal and has all dominion and power over Satan and his kingdom. However, the adversary attempts to counterfeit God's manifestations. A Biblical example of Satan's counterfeiting scheme is when Aaron's rod was cast on the ground before Pharaoh and supernaturally transformed into a serpent. Pharaoh was unimpressed as his two chief magicians, Jannes and Jambres, threw their two rods on the palace floor, transforming them into serpents. These counterfeiters duplicated a powerful miracle.

However, God's snake swallowed up the two serpents of the magicians, leaving them without a god or a rod! Obviously, the purpose of this false miracle was to convince people who were undecided about the God of Moses, by attempting to demonstrate that there was no difference between the God of the Hebrews and the gods of the Egyptians. The counterfeit miracle was to deceive people by making it appear that God and Satan's power are equal, and in doing so, making no distinction between Moses's Deity and the gods of the Egyptians.

In Acts 8, Simon the sorcerer seduced and deceived the people of Samaria through his occult practices. Peter boldly rebuked him after this wicked man offered money to purchase the gift of the laying on of hands (Acts 8:18-23). In the early church, one of the primary spirits that Believers battled in the culture was the spirit of sorcery or magic that was commonly practiced at pagan temples. In the city of Thyatira, Paul encountered a woman with a spirit of divination who was a fortune teller. The word divination in Greek is *puthon*, meaning a spirit of python which was linked to the Greek mythological god Apollo. According to the Greeks, as soon as Apollo was born, he destroyed a serpent named python (Acts 16:16). Paul cast the evil spirit from the woman and she lost her ability to predict the future (Acts 16:18-19).

COUNTERFEIT BLOOD AND RELIGIOUS DAYS

From the two animals slain in the Garden of Eden to the days of the Temple in Jerusalem, numerous forms of animal sacrifices were offered on stone altars throughout the land and on the brazen altar at the Tabernacle and Temple. The blood of the animal sacrifice spoke as a witness of God's power to forgive and atone for sins.

When a patriarch needed God's attention, he would slay an animal and burn the offering upon an altar. The ritual of animal sacrifices was known among the Egyptians, Babylonians, Greeks and Romans. Modern occult rites, such as voodoo, use blood from various animals when pronouncing a curse or attempting to remove a curse from a follower. Among satanists, neopagans and others, blood holds significant power in their religion.

For a Christian, their day of power was the day in which they chose to enter a redemptive covenant through Christ. That is when sin was replaced with forgiveness, and darkness was replaced with light. In Judaism the most significant day is the Day of Atonement, when once a year the High Priest entered the Holy of Holies to make atonement for himself, his fellow priests, and all Israelites. If God saw true repentance, all sin was removed that day. Jewish tradition teaches that on the Day of Atonement, God limits the influence and presence of Satan and his evil spirits as they are banned from the Temple platform on this day. God's forgiveness gave Israel power over all spirits and influence of the adversary on this Day of Atonement.

In Islam, the most important month is Ramadan, the ninth month of the Islamic calendar, believed by Muslims to be the month in which the angel Gabriel revealed the revelations to Mohammad that were later penned in the Koran. The month lasts between twenty-nine and thirty days and is based upon the visual sighting of the moon. Devout Muslims are required to fast from dawn to sunset, including avoiding liquids and sexual relations. They also increase their numbers of prayers and recite additional passages from the Koran.

In Islam there is a "night of power." Islamic scholars teach that the Koran was revealed over a period of twenty-three years, but the night of the first revelation given to Mohammad is considered the night of power. Some Muslims believe the night falls on one of the last ten days of Ramadan, and according to the Haddith (Islamic tradition) is the 27th of the month. Muslims further believe that, on this night, special groups of angels are dispatched to the earth on behalf of Muslims around the world. In the days of Osama bin Laden, the United States government was always on higher alert during the Islamic "night of power," as it was speculated this could be set as a time of major attack, since Muslims believed that angels would be working on behalf of the Islamic world.

In the Hindu religion, which is the predominate religion in India, there are specific seasons believed to introduce special power, especially with the mother goddess. There is also a marked season in which Hindus make a pilgrimage to the river to wash away their sins. When a Hindu converts to Christianity, the Christian pastor will change the new convert's Hindu name to a Christian name, and as a public sign of conversion to Christ, the new Believer must be baptized in water.

Several missionary friends conduct something called the New Moon Crusade in India. There is total darkness during a new moon, which spreads fear of the influence of evil spirits among the Hindu people. The Christian teams will set up huge lights in the night, sing and preach, and often exorcise demonic spirits from the people who are being attacked or possessed by those spirits.

THE OCCULT POWER DAYS

I was unaware of the information I am going to share with you, until I began studying about how the adversary designs his own days as a counter to the holy days of God. There is a pagan religion called Wicca, which is a form of witchcraft that marks certain "high holy days." Various pagan and occult organizations such as this exist, and they might recite incantations, offer some type of prayers, and have a belief that their actions release certain spirits into situations.

Both the longest and the shortest days of the year are marked as significant by pagans and occultists. The longest day is June 21, and the shortest day is December 21. Another set time is April 30 – May 1, known as Bealtain. April 30 was the day in which Hitler is said to have killed himself and had stated that in the future his ghost would return.

One of the main yearly times for these groups is the festival that celebrates the dead, also known as halloween (which was once called samhain). Notice that these two dates are six months apart. These are also two important dates for people within these groups to recruit other followers.

The Apostle Peter used a metaphor to reveal that Satan is like a roaring lion (1 Pet. 5:8). Normally, when Scripture uses an animal metaphor to describe a person or a prophetic empire, it identifies the characteristics of that person or empire that match the characteristics of the animal. There are many interesting facts about lions that also describe our adversary. For example, just as the occult seeks new recruits and converts twice a year, a lion will mate two times a year, about six months apart.

Significant occult dates include:

- February 2nd   - candle mass

- May 1st   - beltaine

- August 1st   - lughnasadh

- September 21st   - mavon

- October 31st   - samhain

- November 1st   - 1st of the year on the occult calendar

Note that May 1st falls between two major Jewish festivals—First Fruits and Pentecost and the counting of the omer. August 1st falls on a timeframe that is often the the seasons of repentance, known as Teshuvah.

Having personally met and heard the testimonies of men and women who, prior to their conversions, were involved in the New Age and other pagan or occult activities, one statement that stands out above others was, "These dates, especially October 31st, are dates with human–demonic interaction." Those heavily involved in these practices believe that the veil between our world and the underworld is the thinnest on October 31st and demons are invited to participate on that day.

The history of halloween is somewhat confusing, but it had its beginnings with a Celtic festival called sow-in, which was the end of the harvest cycle in their culture. This time was recognized in the area of Scotland and Ireland when Celtics took stock of supplies and slaughtered their livestock for winter. Ancient heathen believed that on October 31st, the worlds of the living and the dead overlapped, and the dead could come back and wreak havoc on crops and life. For a few centuries, it has been taught that sow-in was the lord of death, with a modern picture being a skeleton with a sickle called the grim reaper.

The beliefs about October 31st included:

- The spirits of the dead had been confined in the bodies of some animals.

- October 31st (sow-in) brought forth the spirits of the dead to return to their homes.

- Druids (to protect from the dead) took animals in wicker baskets and burned them in bonfires.

When the Roman Empire occupied the nations, the Romans took over and added another part to the celebration in late October, in which they celebrated both the passing of the dead and Pomona, the goddess of fruit. Her symbol was an apple, and herein we find the origin of bobbing for apples on halloween.

The pagan celebration was called all-hallows-eve among the Europeans. Pope Gregory II and Gregory IV moved the old Christian feast called All Saints' Day from May 13th to November 1st (835), one day after halloween.

Numerous traditions developed over time, including dressing up as creatures from the underworld (ghost, witches and zombies). A belief emerged that dead spirits wandered the earth on this night, and food and drink were prepared for them (treats). If the "treats" were not received by the spirits, they would return the following year and play tricks on the person.

A tradition later developed in England, where each November 4th was called "Mischief Night" as children played tricks on people. The idea of a jack-o-lantern originated through a man named Jack who claimed to trick the devil, who was thought to wander the earth and not be in either heaven or hell. The hollowed out pumpkins were cut out with a face to frighten evil spirits.

How did halloween gain a foothold in America? After a great potato famine struck Ireland in the mid-1800s, many Irish immigrants came to America. The traditions surrounding halloween came through the Irish.

An in-depth study will show how halloween is believed to be connected to the spirits of the dead. In reality, these spirits are not the departed souls of loved ones, but are demonic and evil spirits. To many in the occult, halloween night is the strongest night of the year for spirit activity. Satanists establish October 31st as "all demons night," and witches will convene to drink, party, pronounce spells and curses, and conjure up spirits. Satanic crimes and other activities have been noted in communities during this season.

Halloween might seem innocent to many, and millions of dollars are made from costumes, candy and other activities at this time. However, Paul wrote:

> *"What am I saying then? That an idol is anything, or what is offered to idols is anything? Rather, that the things which the Gentiles sacrifice they sacrifice to demons and not to God, and I do not want you to have fellowship with demons. You cannot drink the cup of the Lord and the cup of demons; you cannot partake of the Lord's table and of the table of demons. Or do we provoke the Lord to jealousy? Are we stronger than He?"*
>
> – 1 CORINTHIANS 10:19-22 (NKJV)

SPIRITUAL ATMOSPHERES

Believers have observed that, on this day, there can be an increase in depression, mental oppression, and strange or unexplainable hindrances. There is an increase in weird warfare, and spiritual changes can be felt in the atmosphere.

Many years ago, when my son Jonathan was only ten months old, he was lying on our bed between Pam and me. We were sound asleep and were suddenly awakened with Jonathan choking. I flipped on the lamp, only to see that he was vomiting. After picking him up, we noticed there was blood was on his left and right temples, almost as though someone had taken their thumb and smeared blood on him. We examined every part of his body and found nothing that would have caused the blood.

When I remembered it was halloween night, a spiritual indignation rose up within me like a fire, and I began to rebuke the spirit that was attacking my son. We later learned that, just down the road, someone had killed a dog and drained the blood from its body. This was obviously an occult spirit attempting to attack my son. However, we took spiritual authority over it by using the blood of Jesus!

WHY DOES THE OCCULT WORLD NEED BLOOD?

There have been and still are false religions and religious rituals that believe there is magical power concealed in blood. While many world religions burn oil or incense and offer food to their gods, among the ancients, blood was an important aspect of the rituals. Animals were slain among the ancient Romans to read the liver or to divine the future from certain organs. Voodoo often used the blood of a chicken, or even small amounts of the blood of a person, in an attempt to place a curse or remove an alleged curse from someone. Pagan tribes in Africa actually drink blood during certain rituals. Even the Mayan Indians offered a human sacrifice to appease the gods.

What is there about blood that, throughout history, has been used during certain religious rituals, offerings and sacrifices? We know from the Bible that the Old Testament sacrifices were offered for sin, trespass, and peace offerings. These pointed to the final offering—Christ, who was offered for our sins. But why should other religions use blood?

Perhaps it is because Satan and his cohorts saw the awesome power of blood under the Old Covenant. God cut the skins from two animals in Eden to cover Adam and Eve. The blood of an earthly lamb provided protection for the Hebrew's firstborn when the destroying angel passed through Egypt. The Almighty established an elaborate system of sacrifices and offerings that Israel kept intact for about fifteen hundred years, from Moses until the destruction of the Temple. The blood on the altar stopped the angel of death from striking Jerusalem in David's time. Satan's ultimate defeat, however, was when Christ shed His own blood so that through His blood, redemption's price was paid.

The adversary's obsession with blood might be because the spirit world is not a flesh and blood realm, and no blood is required for an eternal spirit to live. God is a spirit, angels are spirit beings, and today Christ has a glorified body. Adam could have never lived in a fleshly body without blood, because the life of the flesh is in the blood (Lev. 17:11). When Cain killed Abel, the voice of Abel's blood cried out to God. So we see that blood is a powerful force that brings life.

DURING OPPRESSIVE SEASONS

If we are aware of specific days and seasons in which there is an increase in negative spiritual activity, then that day should be covered in more prayer.

There are four seasons of the year, and moving from one season to the next initiates a new season on God's festival calendar. From winter to spring, Israel entered the season of Passover, Unleavened Bread, and First Fruits. From spring we move to summer, where Pentecost is the early summer theme. From summer to fall, Israel entered the seasons of the fall feasts— Trumpets, Atonement and Tabernacles. Fall turns to winter, and winter brings Hanukkah, the Festival of Lights. There is a spiritual application to these seasonal changes. When the seasons change in our lives, spring being the new beginning and winter being our closing days on earth, we must encounter the Presence of God with each seasonal transition.

Being an exile in Babylon, the prophet Daniel understood spiritual battles over the atmosphere of this pagan nation where he and his companions had been confined. In Jerusalem there was a morning and evening sacrifice. In Babylon Daniel prayed not twice, but three times a day, increasing his personal intercession, despite a law forbidding him to pray to his God. On another occasion, his understanding of a vision was being hindered by a strong demonic prince, causing Daniel to initiate a twenty-one day fast to break the power of the hindering spirit in the heavens (see Daniel 10).

The authority of the Prince of Persia to restrain an angel of the Lord and withhold the answer to Daniel's prayer for three weeks indicates that invisible, yet real satanic forces can blanket a region in the second heaven and make the atmosphere like a brass sheet. Answers to prayer do not penetrate the earthly atmosphere from the third heaven easily in these cases.

Fasting, prayer, and the release of a stronger angel named Michael pierced the dark veil, until finally an angel of God arrived with the light and illumination Daniel was seeking.

The fact that Daniel interceded three weeks for his breakthrough shows us that the power of intercessory prayer is the key to breaking through the demonic seasons we encounter in life. The Daniel narrative also illustrates the importance of angelic messengers who will assist Believers during times of serious spiritual warfare. At times it takes a spirit (angel) to defeat a spirit (Satan). Remember that angels are assigned to minister to those who shall be the heirs of righteousness (Heb. 1:7).

CHAPTER 14

THE ULTIMATE PURPOSE
OF PROPHETIC CODES

FOUR IMPORTANT AND significant phrases in Scripture are connected with prophetic time. I identify *prophetic time* as specific moments on an earthly timeline where the predictions of Biblical prophets and apostles are clearly being fulfilled.

In Scripture various phrases are used to identify prophetic time. Christ spoke to His disciples of the times and seasons which the Father had in His power (Acts 1:7). Daniel coined a phrase, "the time of the end," found in five passages of his book (Dan. 8:17; 11:35, 40; 12:4, 9). A third phrase also used in Daniel is his reference to, "at the time appointed" (Dan. 8:19; 10:1; 11:27, 29, 35). There is also a term in the New Testament coined by the Apostle Paul, "the fullness of times" (Eph. 1:10). What are the meanings of these phrases?

First we must understand time. The world views time as a linear flow. Men are able to flow and move through both time and space. Ancient earthly time was counted by the yearly and monthly cycles of the sun and moon, whereas, today clocks count time. Earthly time can be compared to a straight time line, which began at the moment Adam fell into sin. People were then marked with a set time, beginning with their birth and concluding with their death.

Earthly time, where human government is controlling the affairs of men, has a set time frame to operate and will cease their control when Christ returns to set up His kingdom for a thousand years. At the conclusion of the thousand years, and following the Great White Throne Judgment, time will be no more, and eternity will initiate a timeless rule for ages upon ages without end.

Earthly time has a beginning and an ending. Prophetic time however, is best described as a circle. Or as some rabbis describe, a spiral circle that moves upward toward God, with a beginning that marks specific prophetic events on the circle. Over time, events move into a full circle, or a fullness of time. As the circle of prophetic time starts over again, the events of the past are often repeated in some form in the future. Solomon indicated this when he wrote:

> "That which is has already been, and what is to be has already been; and God requires an account of what is past."
>
> – ECCL. 3:15 (NKJV)

> "That which has been is what will be, that which is done is what will be done, and there is nothing new under the sun. Is there anything of which it may be said, 'See, this is new?' It has already been in ancient times before us."
>
> – ECCL. 1:9-10 (NKJV)

If we break down the four phrases found in Scripture, the *times and seasons* are God's pre-planned prophetic events on the cyclical time line. When we reach the specific season of time for that event to occur, it will unfold on the exact point where God marked its fulfillment in the beginning.

The time of *the end* is where the ancient prophetic signs of the final days emerge in one time frame, as human government climaxes and eventually ends on the circle of time. The Messiah begins His rule with a new time marker of a thousand years, fulfilling Messianic Kingdom predictions (Dan. 2:44; 7:27).

The appointed times are the specific pre-determined seasons and events that are marked on the timeline.

The fullness of *times* is when all things come full circle and total fulfillment occurs. For example, Christ ascended from the Mount of Olives, and will return to the Mount of Olives (Acts 1:11; Zech. 14:4).

Even the Hebrew word for year—shana—has a double meaning of both repetition and change.

From Adam to the end of the one-thousand-year reign of Christ is the human timeline. On this line God, from the beginning of time, set the specific day for the flood of Noah, the birth of Isaac, the Hebrews coming out of Egyptian captivity, the birth of Christ, and His crucifixion and resurrection. This line of time will end after the new heaven and new earth are created and the New Jerusalem comes down from heaven to earth (Rev. 21:1-2). There will be no need for time; and time as we know it will be no more.

Christ calls Himself the "beginning and the end" three times in Revelation (1:8; 21:6; 22:13). Yet Christ had no beginning and no end, as He pre-existed with God who had no beginning or end. This "beginning" is explained in Revelation 3:14, where Christ states that He is "the faithful and true witness, the beginning of the creation of God."

From an earthly perspective, Christ's beginning was His earthly birth, and the earthly end will come when He halts human, earthly government and initiates His eternal kingdom. This period between the beginning of creation and the end of human government is called time. Time is an interruption of eternity, and eternity is timeless.

The feasts were yearly celebrations that centered around rain and the harvest. The cycles of the sun determined the year, as it took 365.25 days for the earth to make a complete circle around the sun. The earth would begin a new circle and a new year for the next 365 days, coming back to the same position and repeating the cycle each year. The feasts were celebrated on the same days and months each year. Calendar adjustments were required to maintain the feasts in their proper circle of time. As the earth made its circle, the moon would enter four phases, creating the months.

God's appointed festivals were celebrated each year in a cyclical fashion, as annual events, the same day and month each year. However, in the prophetic circle, certain parallel events would repeat throughout history on the same days as the set festivals and set seasons of God—on the very months or days designated as God's appointed seasons.

Christ the Lamb of God was crucified near Passover (John 19:14), and the church was born on the Feast of Pentecost (Acts 1:1-4). The return of the Lord and many future prophetic events will repeat themselves on the Jewish festival days. Even in the Millennial reign, the Feast of Tabernacles will be celebrated each year for a thousand years during Christ's rule (Zech. 14:16-19).

This is why, at times, previous historical patterns repeat in history with such accuracy. The difficulty with patterns is that they have many cross-connections. Yet, certain past narratives in the Bible are specifically repeated in the life or redemptive ministry of Christ. The importance of tapping into Biblical patterns is that all humans are created to learn through continuous exposure to patterns. Even speaking is learned by repeating continual and consistent patterns. Many forms of work are learned through repetitive patterns.

The weakness of many theologians, in my opinion, is to over-analyze words, phrases and comparisons to arrive at a set conclusion. There is no need to do this, because after all, the Bible was written by common men to common people and not to advanced theologians to dissect, debate, and argue over every verse. We can take three different scholars from three different denominations, and each will arrive at three different conclusions from the same passages of Scripture. One will prove that God is still a healer today. Another will read the same verses and conclude that God healed in the New Testament, but He does not manifest healing today. Yet a third will say that the healing manifestation today is spiritual and not physical healing.

There is a circle of prophecy, and the revelation of the Messiah and the covenant is concealed within the stories of Abraham and Isaac (Gen 22), the serpent on the pole (Num. 21), and the burning of a red heifer, (Num. 19), all within the Old Testament. These patterns of prophecy will remain concealed and simply ancient narratives until we dig them out in their layers.

As prophetic time spirals toward eternity, our next major appointed meeting is the time we are changed from mortality to immortality at the moment of the gathering together (1 Cor. 15:51-53). By understanding the cyclical flow of prophetic movements and events, patterns emerge that reveal how major prophecies can and will be fulfilled during the major feasts of Israel, specifically the fall feasts.

In summary, the three fall feasts are Trumpets, Atonement, and Tabernacles—three festivals that reveal the three main prophetic events that will occur in the future, according to the New Testament. Trumpets is the imagery of the gathering together of the church, followed by the tribulation judgments pictured in the Day of Atonement. Following the tribulation, we come to the thousand-year Kingdom of the Messiah, which is pictured in the Feast of Tabernacles. God established these festivals for practical and prophetic purposes, and they conceal the future of mankind, the church, and the coming Kingdom!

NOTES

NOTES

NOTES

NOTES

NOTES

NOTES

NOTES

NOTES